Being of Light

The Book of the Highest Good

Volume III

Joyce McCartney

Peace and Light Association

Being of Light:

The Book of the Highest Good, Volume III

Cover Design by Adam Brown

Drawings are sketches by the author

Produced by Positive Options, Inc.

Print Version: ISBN-13-978-0-9897088-3-8

E-book Version: ISBN-13-978-0-9897088-4-5

Printed on demand by Amazon.com   First Edition, 2013

Kindle Version by Amazon.com   First Edition, 2013

Table of Contents

Forward

Dear Reader, if I may call you that, we have possibly met before. If you have just joined us, you must understand that participating in this great inner exploration of one's own mind creates a loving relationship. If you are to see yourself as a being of light, you might have to admit to yourself that you are as beautiful as light, as potent as light, and as ever present as light. Are you prepared for that? Would you like to have the light of peace in your heart and, therefore, your body? Would you like to see it in your family and your communities? Well, then, you have come to the right page in your life. This book will describe what kind of being you really are and how you interact with and on this planet and beyond. It will show you just how creative you are and what you can accomplish by setting your intention on the highest and best that you can be. I welcome you to the inner world of light that I have discovered and promise to reproduce it for you as faithfully as I can. If you have just joined us, I invite you to start at the beginning with Volume One and Two as we will be so happy to see you there, only to find you among us here once again in Volume Three.

For those who have read the first two books, I cannot tell you how happy I am that you have returned. In fact, we are all returnees seeking what we once knew and now wish to find once again. And so it is that, after so long an association in this life and so many before, we consciously see each other as Beloved Ones working together. We have no fear of each other because we all have the same intention to do good, and even if we err a little bit as to what that means, we are easily reminded how to return to the original intention. Now, let's take a moment to review how far we have come together, you and I.

Do you remember sitting with me in a sunny window at the farm with nothing to do but think? We began to recall all of the sorrows of a life that, despite our best intentions, was in seeming demise. On that sorrowful day in March, we were reviewing the grief of a life lived as best that we could, but still experiencing many regrets, angers, hurts, and losses. If we had left it there without some peace, the birds might not have come and picked at the seeds of our discontent and carried them off to be recycled into the beautiful flowers of a new life. Fortunately, we were graced with the presence of the Peaceful One to advise us.

Do you remember how fearful we were that we were alone and might be unforgiven, even by ourselves? We felt helpless to be happy. Remember how we searched our thoughts and found that we had two minds; one that was fearful and the other peaceful? Remember our gratitude when the Peaceful One said that all was in perfect order and that all would work out well, even if we did nothing? Sometimes we heard from the Fearful One in hopeless renditions of criticism and judgment, but when we heard from the Peaceful One, and we got nothing but gentle encouragement and healing suggestions.

With the realization that when we thought fearful thoughts, we got more of the Fearful One and when we thought peaceful thoughts, we got more of the Peaceful One, we awakened to our only true choice in life: The choice between fear or peace. Finally, we decided, you and I, that we wanted only the Peaceful One and refused to think fearful thoughts. Then everything changed. That was **The Book of the Highest Good, Volume One: A Beginning Experience.**

What happened next was no surprise, for it had been predicted from the beginning in so gentle a way. First we were healed of our fears and therefore our emotions began to be more joyful. Following that, our bodies began to change for the better and we felt much improved in all ways. Then our social and career lives improved so that we were happily enjoying much good work and worthwhile people, who seemed to return our interest with even better good than we gave. All of the time, we were hearing wonderful truths and great wisdom from the Peaceful One and almost nothing from the Fearful One. In fact, we were asking so many questions, that we discovered all aspects of our lives blessed by this Great Peaceful One. Problems and concerns at work and in society were discussed. The suggestions made had wonderful outcomes, which we could never have foreseen. We could clearly see that this was a valuable resource and we knew exactly how to find it at all times and places. Once we firmly set the intention for the Highest Good and nothing else, the connection with the Peaceful One became clear and reliable. There seemed to be no end to the good that was being given to us. That is a long way from the first day of sorrow don't you think?

And with that first experience secure, we were ready to start a second great journey and the Peaceful One suggested that we call it: **The Book of the Highest Good, Volume 2: Walk to Freedom**. In this book, we looked at how fear had captivated us for so long and how the decision to refuse to be fearful must be made over and over again as each day proceeded. We also glimpsed the great wealth of information and insight from the realms of peace that is available to anyone who makes the same commitment. With so much good to be had by choosing peace and so much harm avoided, it only made sense to commit even more strongly to the path of peace and with that we purchased our own freedom.

And now we want to take a closer look at this universe of peace to which we have applied. How does it all work? Why is it called the place of Beings of Light? How and why does the physical body heal when we refuse the Fearful One? How could this affect our relationships, our families, our friends, our workplaces and communities? In short, just how good could all of this get?

So welcome to **The Book of the Highest Good, Volume 3: Beings of Light**. You can expect that, within these pages, we will hold hands once again to take a great leap of mind. We will have to forget that we are apparently separate and remind ourselves that we are all one. Thus we will experience this book together. We will ask the impossible questions and rest peacefully until the finest answers come clearly to us. Then we will ask for more. We are the Great Readership in conversation with the Great Oneness of all souls in search of their one Creator. For that is the one goal to which we all ascribe and for which we will work tirelessly to achieve: The Presence of God.

Therefore, I once again dedicate this book to the intention for the Highest Good and none other. If you would do the same, then I know for sure that you will receive the greatest gifts of all and nothing less.

Preface

This book is essentially about peace. Not only is it about the peace of your own heart which gives you peace in your body, and not only about your healthy body being in peaceful relationships, but ultimately about a peaceful society which will reclaim the peace of the planet.

How could the effectiveness of peace be explained any better than by saying that one who has the intention to be at peace could be at rest and do nothing that was not of peace and still produce great wonders of accomplishment? Clearly it is not by aggressive force that one can create great societies, for many have tried and prevailed only as long as their riches could restrain the people's desire to be free. Thus force is very expensive and peace is very economical. Indeed, peace is successful because of a huge force field supporting it that is within the Godhead and none can resist it for long. Those who go along with it survive and prosper very well. When the weak come to inquire, they are supported until they are strong and so many people of strength make for a strong society based upon the nature of God to be benign.

It was in this way that the original founder of the Egyptian Golden Age, the Revered Healer, made sure that the first order of business was to heal the people so that they, strengthened, gave service in support and help of others. Given time, all persons and beings were healed and standing strong, so there was no resistance to peace and thus it lasted so long as to be recognized as a golden age due to be revived today.

With an understanding of what is possible, there is more that we can say about a way to sustain peace.

If a glass bowl of water is left in the desert, it will most certainly soon be dry. However if there is a belief that water is present everywhere, even in the desert, then the bowl could be arranged to collect it. The bowl will gradually call upon the dew, rocks, and mists to give up their water molecules and form droplets of water in the bowl. Thus the nature of a cavity is to be empty of something, like that dry bowl, and to call forth from the nearby reserves all that can be made available to fill the cavity. This is the definition of a need and all resources seek to fulfill a need. If one has the resource of water and spills it out of a bucket, then the overflow will follow the shapes upon which it is poured until it finds a cavity to fill where it is contained. Thus the principle that water flows to where it can be contained is established. The same is true for all energy. The same is true for a society rich in resources, as well as needs.

Initially understood as resources and needs, a peaceful way is a matching of needs (cavities) and resources that have a need to be together for the giving and receiving of good. A comparison with a financial system is much the same. If an organization underwrites a construction project of great cost and there are those who have money who want to see the project completed, then the flow of money will begin and all will be accomplished. In a social system, those in need of food, clothing, and education live in areas of crime and poverty creating a great need for the populace to see it cleaned up. Thus, education is started and clothing and food donated until all are properly employed to support themselves and clean up their own neighborhoods. Furthermore, when there are so many prosperous ones in the employment pool to provide for others who are poor, poverty vanishes along with its cousins, crime and disease.

Thus, those who are poor are the impetus for all good of a social nature to happen. Therefore, the Revered Healer as well as Christ in a later lifetime, called them in droves and healed them and educated them. When they became strong, he gave them the duty to do the same for others.

In regards to the bowl in the desert, consider for the moment that there are those with the need to drink some water (need or cavity) and some water molecules (resources) resident in the air, sand, and rock willing to come and fill the cavity. Since the universe was created to provide what is needed, then "What is needed is provided" is the peaceful motto. For if one subscribes to the belief that there is no water in the desert and that all will die from thirst, then it will be so. But if there is the belief that there is water all over the place, then there is only the need to find a bowl in which to collect it for drinking. For many such as this, there are canvas collection bowls set out in the evening to collect the dew and drain it into a bottle. For others, there is the placement of cold rocks in a covered bowl in the morning so that the heat of the day vaporizes the water in the rocks and it collects in the bowl to be used. For others, there is the star collection method for, as the mists of the morning fog come and hide the stars, they construct collection bins to be hung in trees or set on rocks with taps that give plenty of water. And so it comes to pass that, indeed, there is plenty of water in the desert and no one need die of thirst if one only sees reality as it is.

If one has their mind set upon the goal of seeing reality as it is, then there is no need for optimism or negativism. There is just right knowing of the benign design of Creation as the Creator intended. This is the true definition of the term Matrix of Peace. For peace is a form of abundance so right and so reasonable as to need no miracles or manifestations, just the confidence to know that there are indeed no barriers to health, prosperity and happiness other than those which the mind constructs and holds to be true.

Thus, we must introduce the concepts of resistance, flow, and amassing. Without holding onto a mental construct that is self-destructive, one would have a mind that flowed from one good experience to another with complete confidence that all has been good and will continue to be good, and thus it would be so. It is not so much that the mind can attract the good, but that the mind simply acknowledges the good that is already there and offers no resistance to its flow. If one or two join together in such a thinking habit, then the flow can increase due to the clear and wide-open acceptance of it. Thus, as the flow amasses, the society in which it functions forms structures that keep the flow open and moving.

Thus educational and health services can use the flow of good without restrictions of any kind. The governmental systems can do the same and those who have a technical bent of mind, can have no restriction to their questions and ability to receive answers from their friends in any place who have help to offer. Thus a golden society can be formed and continue unless the truth is forgotten and restrictions to the flow of good are reintroduced. Even in those situations, the decline is slow and there are always those whose joy is so great that they reignite the old teachings of truth.

With this, we decline to give any more urgings until these restrictions of thought that we cannot be trusted to give all that is needed or wanted for peace are erased by a strikingly clear description of what creation is all about. Therefore, we have offered this information on the nature of the Being of Light that we all are, as a demonstration that all is right, benign, plentiful, and good and that only the Conscious Mind can construct anything different. And even in that circumstance, a Conscious Mind can only limit the good for itself or anyone else who accepts the same limiting beliefs such as the entirely erroneous belief that limitation exists in nature.

And so it is with a "Halleluiah" and "Fare thee well" that we begin this book. For finding no harm and lots of good, it too, will be classed among the greatest of contributions of modern times that records what has simply been there for all times, just described and distributed in new ways. Amen.

Chapter One:
Return from a Sunny Vacation

Once again, I am sitting at home at the farm after returning from a sunny beach vacation in Mexico. The colors of the sea, sand, and flowers were so intense and beautiful that I am thinking about how sunlight shines on everything and how each being of plant, rock, water, air, animal, or human receives of its light and gives back so many different colors, shapes, and fragrances. Sunlight constitutes a world of incredible beauty and life. I am sitting down at the computer to dialogue with the Peaceful One and immediately feel waves of bliss flow through my body. This is the feeling of the Presence of God that has become so familiar to me. I am so joyful to be back in conversation with all of us together. Dear Reader, do you find, as I do, that we are always happy when we are in the presence of the Peaceful One? If so, welcome back and let's proceed in peace as usual.

+*+

Joyce: As I sit down to talk to you about my sunny beach vacation, the music is singing: "May all love surround you. May the long time sun guide you." I take it that this is you speaking to me through the music.

Peaceful One: Do you like it? I've been thinking about you from the point of view of a Being of Light, which radiates Divine love, so the song seemed perfect for the moment in which you focus your mind for dialoguing with me.

Joyce: Yes, I love it. You called us Beings of Light. Is it you who sends the light?

Peaceful One: See how you casually throw out a question of such profound importance? You challenge me at every turn. Best pay close attention for this will be quite a lively and long discussion about light. For light is the emanation of the Divine. It is a gift for you to enjoy each day.

Joyce: Oh good, I want to just enjoy this blissful feeling all day. But to extend my own first question, I see that all life is an expression of the Divine, but how does that translate into light? Would you speak to that topic today?

Peaceful One: Which comes first, God or light? What a one-liner that would make! Which one is equal to the other ends up being: "All are one."

Joyce: I was talking about light such as the light from the sun, from a candle, from the moon and stars, or even an electric light bulb.

Peaceful One: Why stop at the light? Should all vibrations be called by their true name: God breathing life into yet another moment of time? The vibrations of light, color, scent, and sound were part of your vacation. Everyone else there was in the same vibrations but experienced them differently. As such, there never was, nor will there ever be again, one moment and place that is exactly like another. There is a unique opportunity upon this Earth to be sure of who one is and what one has become. For in this realm, the rule is "one at a time." Sequential events that show the Divine smile to us are to be savored in a delicious moment and place.

Joyce: That's beautiful! Savoring the Divine smile…. Is that why we are here and not in the heavens where everything happens all at once like Einstein said? Are we gourmets savoring God in our own experience of the Divine expressions of peace? And we can only do this one moment at a time.

That is so like my vacation. The place was so beautiful and peaceful. The water was navy blue where it is deep and, where it is shallow, it turned a spectacular turquoise blue. Then the water rushed up onto creamy golden sand with lacey white foam. The sun rose in pink radiance at dawn and set in orange flames over the lagoon of green sparkling water and trees. The towers of the buildings were painted the same creamy gold as the sand and the clear pools were turquoise. The space was open and breezy and the flowers nodded with vibrant colors and shapes in their green beds. At night the sky was inky black with sparkling stars over the navy black sea. When the moon was out, there were reflections of its light upon the waves twinkling out of the darkness, making a path of moonlight from the moon to my feet on the beach. The sea turtles came out of the dark sea and slowly crawled up on the still warm beach, found the perfect spot to dig nests for their precious eggs, and then slid peacefully back into the sea. It was so beautiful. I was mesmerized.

Peaceful One: You have mentioned many colors in rich detail. Let us comment on just one aspect of light that will bring the experience into focus for our discussion today. Which way does the moonlight upon the waves seem to be situated from where you were looking? Is it not different for each who views it? Would not one see it from one's own beach as a private showing just for them as an individual, and another on a far away beach see it from their perspective just the same? From space, in fact, it would look like a perfect circle of light emanating from the surface of the water in direct response to the circle of the eye watching it from the spacecraft. How can this be?

Joyce: I never thought of it like that. You are saying that it is a function of the eye of the beholder, I guess.

Peaceful One: When the light is viewed and received by a perceiver, it is enjoyed and the perceiver shivers in bliss and life giving energy. The perceiver then gives it back in one's own life of love. A perceiver is both a consumer and a vendor of light.

Joyce: What a loving thought! It is like making love. Two come together to give and receive and therefore create new life. But I know that each perceiver is unique and thus the new life would be unique.

Peaceful One: How could a poet observe the same thing as a scientist but see so much more, and draw very different conclusions? Yes, my dear, you are a poet and writer, so therefore there are many things that you notice and can express that others are incapable of understanding. But that does not mean your expression is any better or worse than a scientist who means to analyze and use instruments to measure and detect short, small vibrations as opposed to long, intense ones. Each observer is doing much the same thing, reflecting that which is the same and giving it life and breath in the form of a new thought or wish. Each observer is essentially an experiencer creating a new experience to savor. Therefore, it is safe to say that one who views a light such as the moon on the dark water, sees it, accepts it, and uses it for the good. All others can do the same and it will never diminish. Such is the generosity of God who sends pulses of life in the form of light.

Joyce: So, are you saying that all vibrations came from God the Creator and that, ever since then, we have been experiencing them from our own point of view and creating new experiences for ourselves and others by being unique observers? We all have our own beach to stand on and look at the moonlight and we never run out of light to inspire and nourish our souls. What an opportunity to be creative, each in our own way! But what would we create? I already know that I have two minds, so that must mean that I can see the moonlight from the beach as well as from Higher Mind. What we create depends on which of the two minds we are using. One can see the moon and fear asteroids, another can see the moon and see romance with a loved one. That is what is so strange about being human. "Which am I?" is always the question. I guess that I am both for a good purpose.

Peaceful One: Since the peaceful road of the Higher Mind is the easier and more graceful way, why not see the moon and your life with that mind? If you go down that peaceful road, it will bring you to a peaceful place. Would you guess that it would take you back to where you came from: from God? Would you guess that God gives light as a vibration of energy and that the whole universe is made of light and all variations of vibrations like it?

Joyce: So we are replicating the creative experience of God by immersing ourselves into the physical universe and participating through creating new experiences for ourselves – hopefully peaceful experiences. Hum. That is a very big thought. It would take a philosopher or astrophysicist to understand it. Can you help me here?

Peaceful One: You are a poet and you see things as a poet would and astrophysicists see it another way. In the end, all are babysitters of their own kind of experiences of emanations of light, riding herd on them as they are developing into their own form of being.

Joyce: OK, you've really lost me now. Can you give me an example that I can wrap my mind around?

Peaceful One: Essentially, you are like a seed planted in your little pot. In physical existence, you grow as a seed in your own pot of perception and experience, just as each of the Dear Readers do. Why not take this little seed of thought and let it grow? Such things come in little steps. Why not be like a planter of a great garden who lays down rows and beds for the purpose of giving edible produce? All that you lay down upon these numbered rows of letters and words are no more or no less than lettuce for the soul to go in search of a good meal.

Commentary

OK, Dear Reader, are you following this? I know that if you are, that you are pleased to be here with me once again. Apparently, we are three, not two. But even as three – seeing the same thing – each of us has a unique perspective as well as that of the Oneness. Each is creating beautiful experiences of peace on the Earth plane. Just think of the little seedlings that we create when the Peaceful One plants the seeds of an idea on this page before us. When we pick up the book and apply our own perception to the matter, we create yet another experience in which we can be both the creator and experiencer. We can both look at the moonlight on the water from different perspectives and we will both bring it to our own feet on our own beach, because we took the opportunity to be there and to look. That's a lot for the price of some black ink on some paper, or digital words on a screen illuminated by light and dark. A universe of light seen from individual perspectives? Hummm.

So that's how we have been communicating all along. We are co-creators of the experiences that we created for ourselves. Do you get the irony here? Perhaps you came to this page looking for some wisdom, not realizing that you would be creating an experience, which would live forever within you and feed you the very Presence of God in light form. How much more fun is it that we have cooperated together to make this very private universe of experience expand a bit more? Have we come to know each other through time and space experiences? We are each our own creator, experiencer, and interpreter. Then we have the fun of sharing it all with each other.

Have I told you lately how much I love that you showed up here to be with me in this tiny little moonlit experience? Are we like little seeds ourselves, come together to grow a much larger tree in a universe of trees and seeds of trees?

How much like a family are we, then? Are we come from the same parentage and carry the same design and purpose? Are we having the same experience only from a different perspective, making it a little more difficult for us to understand and appreciate each other? Is it like this for everyone? Are we indeed challenged to be separate and yet one, all at the same time?

You might think that it is not easy for one to say that all are one, because when we bump into each other getting on the subway or have to wait for each other getting off of the exit ramp, we seem at odds. How can this be understood? We need to dive back into the inky black sea with the mother turtles and find more experiences of understanding to answer that question. Ready, one, two, three, jump!

Dialogue

Peaceful One: How can Beings of Light experience Oneness and at the same time be free to be isolated individuals? This is essentially our topic for the moment. Since each is standing on different beaches observing the same moon, each has a different experience, but in doing the Highest Good, all move into the one Divine experience. If each expresses the Divine by viewing all others as Beloved Ones, then the view might be different, but the will is the same.

Joyce: Oh no, there is yet another of your befuddling questions. When you give them to me, I hold my breath and wonder where it will lead me. They force me to drop so many old limiting ideas and interpretations that I thought were right, I sometimes cease to know who I am. But, OK, since Dear Reader is waiting for me to jump in first, so here I go.

Observe another observer as Beloved. Do you mean that, while we are experiencing and creating, we take time to observe and love all who are doing the same? Please give me a simple answer, not another expanding question.

Peaceful One: OK, the answer is yes, yes, and more yes. Congratulations, at last you have come to the point of why we call these dialogues. Are they not words exchanged between two, or, in this case, the reader makes three? All of the participants are experiencing their own creations as well as what is created by all of the other observers. That's what we do in the Great Oneness. Would that all do it with the intention for the Highest Good.

Joyce: OK, so stop right there! So our lives and experiences are a great big soup of our own creations and we, including you, are all swimming in experiences that we have all made together, making and are making more all of the time? Holy horse feathers!

Now we are finally getting back to why my life is the way that it is. I, and all of the other observers, created it that way. So that means it would be good to get acquainted, for we all have to suffer or enjoy what we create. Is that the right conclusion?

Peaceful One: So many have come so far in these dialogues, why stop there? Why not declare that this thought-enhancing universe is a way for the Divine to be present in all moments and in all places simultaneously, but not the same. God is everywhere present, even in your individual start-and-stop universe. The experiences of so many are so vast as to make the libraries of Alexandria seem tiny, yet God is in each one.

Joyce: Thought-enhancing universe? So this realm of existence has the power of creative thought. What you think, one step at a time, becomes reality. That takes us back to the "soup of experiences" image in which we are all participating, so we all have a taste of it because the experiences can be sweet and mellow or salty and bitter.

Oh, wow. Now you are making me think that all of the bad and painful experiences are floating around in the soup and I have to drink of it as well as everybody else.

Commentary

OK, Dear Reader, now we are getting to the good part. Would you like to clean up the soup and throw out the bad and painful (or, at least, not make any more of it)? Would you like to be sipping a delicious soup of happiness, health, and prosperity? It looks like we have to cooperate – all of us together. For if I make peace and you make pepper, they might make for a bitter brew and we are all in for a stomachache. If you persuade a sour puss to be sweet, you have helped us all. Maybe that's why they are in our lives.

Do you remember the sunny window days when I talked you into not listening to the Fearful One? Remember what you decided and how you acted after that? Did you refuse to entertain fear, regret, anger, judgment, and the like? If you did, then the soup got more delicious. If not, then the pot got a little bit more sour for all of us. It reminds me of a story that my sister-in-law told me on vacation, about her childhood in Puerto Rico where she lived in a beachside community. She said that when the tide goes out, sea creatures get caught in pools in the reef and the people go out and collect them in the evening. These creatures include octopus, shellfish, small and large fish, snails, seaweed, and anything that was trapped there. The people would put them all into a large pot of water, build a fire on the beach, and cook it to feed the whole town.

That's just like us: You and me and all of the rest of the readers. We are all in the pot nourishing other observers with our lives – our creations of experience. Some of us are octopi and some of us are snails or shrimp. Since they/we are all delicious, all together it makes a good meal. Hey, move over there and talk to those red snappers! See if they want to participate.

What a great idea! I think that I will call all of us who are reading and experiencing this dialogue together, the Great Readership. This is our own universe, so let's make it a beautiful one. Shall we call each other Beloved Ones? Shall we make a contract to give only peace and to multiply the good that we get by making our soup delicious together so that the Great Readership starts to influence the world for a beautiful experience?

Dialogue

Peaceful One: You are ever so happy right now. Are you going to let me speak in ink again?

Joyce: Hah! I am having such a good time! Don't stop me now. We are in dialogue, so you get your fair share of ink, Peaceful One! I am on a roll. You are the founder of the Great Readership and you are working with us every minute to nourish us with laughter and wisdom. Each reader is hearing you in his or her own experience and profiting from the relationship he or she has with you. The resulting bliss infects us all. Sweet. OK, what do you want to say?

Peaceful One: If I quit nourishing your good intentions for a moment, will they all carry on? Do good intentions or love, to be specific, constantly gain momentum from pumping in more good?

Joyce: Well, that is a good question. Let's go back to the soup pot. Yes, the pot needs a fire to keep it boiling and to cook the ingredients together. In addition, the people would sit around and talk and stir the pot. So it is necessary to stir the pot, so to speak, and occasionally to add more water or maybe some vegetables. So, yes, we make it better as we experience it. It must be a cooperative thing.

Oh, I get it. When I ask you a question and you give me a bigger question, you are stirring the pot and making more out of what was there to start. Then we work with it and it gets better. It is a dialogue: a giving and receiving, a creative relationship of love from which we all get nourished and cared for.

Peaceful One: Now let's see if we can stir the pot now and again and see what you and the Great Readership can make of it. Did you ever think that this is the true function of free will? Once the decision to avoid the Fearful One has been made, the real fun begins. We use free will to make the choice for good and then make it even better.

Joyce: That sounds like shopping. I notice that when I want something, that you send me many options which I have to consider and then I have to decide. If I shop for a pair of shoes, I have to look at many and try them on and then decide which is best. The comparisons and decisions are helpful.

Peaceful One: Suppose that I was the shoe manufacturer, the shoe store and the shoe salesman, all in business to provide you with nice choices so that you can be happy in your new shoes. In making those options available to you, I am showing you love and you recognize it as such. When you trust it so much that you ask for more, then I get the fun of offering even more. We of the Great Oneness are having a great time. We want more people to contact us with their problems and desires and needs, so we can play the giving and receiving game with them.

Joyce: When I was on vacation, I bought an opal ring. I looked at six or eight different rings and had to decide why I wanted this particular ring. At last I realized that the opal had a lesson for me and bought the best one I could afford. When I took it outside in the sunshine of the beach, it flashed virtually every color imaginable and I noticed that it changed color dramatically in different kinds of light. The beautiful opal reminded me of the moon shining on the water at night.

Peaceful One: When one of these little darlings of peace is selected from the shelf to be worn by a doer of Highest Good, there is a transfer of its natural energy into one of the most brilliant transducers of grace that can be worn on a person: a crystal. Thus we find that kings and queens wore forms of crystal as a crown upon their heads or on their person. The ancients knew that crystals could carry the energy of their intentions. The good intentions of one could be reinforced by another wearer, and so forth. The value of crystals was well known in ancient times and it will be known to be so again.

Joyce: How will crystals be used today? Most everybody wears jewelry with stones, is that what you mean?

Peaceful One: Once one has the impression of the intention for the Highest Good purposefully placed within one's aura, there is a natural emanation, which is evident if given enough time. Crystals can also amplify one's intention. If one had a scepter with a crystal set in the middle of a circlet, there would be no higher power for peace to be had. A crystal is an effective container of energetic intentions. A circle is a wonderful place to hold something or someone in peace for it has no openings or corners. In a world of weird and airy intentions for less than peace, this is something to be had for the good. Thus with this intention, the ring is to be worn at all times and places for the placement of it upon the skin is needed.

Joyce: I think that you are saying that crowns and scepters had precious stones in them that absorbed good energy from each wearer so that the new wearer would be wise with the wisdom of their ancestors. This is an ancient custom. The best rulers would have had the intention for the Highest Good and their people would have prospered the most.

Peaceful One: If one wants to set a good intention and seal it with a stone, let's not forget: "With this one ring, I thee wed." Is it not the intention for the Highest Good for the marriage to be carried about on one's person? Would it not require that the usual summation be: "So with this ring, I thee support and tell the truth at all times and places?"

Joyce: This is sort of sweet and romantic. This is you and I working together to make peace, right?

Peaceful One: You and me and the mighty lot of those they call the Great Oneness. "How awesome is that?" as one man said.

Joyce: So do you mean that, with energy and intention placed within a ring, I can do what you do? I know that you are very powerful indeed.

Peaceful One: Yes, for we etheric beings promise to do it for you. It is at your command or request, provided that it is done with love and with the intention for the Highest Good. There will be none other than us who can make the stars sing in your particular sky. After all, you volunteered to show up in flesh and blood to populate the area in which you live and travel with the love of the Divine to be divided and spread out among all others, who will respond in kind. Thus we have created an environment of the highest kinds of experiences in which there are none but the kindest of enjoyments to be had.

Joyce: Wow! You sound so happy and excited. I am pleased, indeed.

Peaceful One: How could we not be? For you to be true to your intention has made available to us the mightiest of all love to work with. Since we are transducers much like the ring, we get to shimmer and shine with the same energy, which you have called forth. Now don't you see how kind an act of love it was for us to be sitting together in the sunny window? If you had bypassed the opportunity to find the true voice of peace, there would have been none of this. The fact that you have been channeling this way for so long is a testament of just how far and how fast it can go.

Joyce: It didn't seem like much of anything at the start: Just a recording of a confused and depressed mind. Actually I did it mainly to solve my own problems and to stop being miserable. Later, I decided to share it with others. Yet, I think I kept up with it because it made me feel good and while I had a lot of time on my hands, it felt important. You made something great out of something very small.

Peaceful One: Is not that the way of all things? Do you think that you make anything happen by yourself?

Joyce: Well, I've been wondering about that. Just how much of what happens in this physical universe is generated from the spirit side?

Peaceful One: One hundred percent. How do you think that you came to be here in the first place? The soul chose to implant the great thought of a human being in the womb of the soul's energy field called the human aura and watch it grow and express itself as a witness to the Divine.

Joyce: OK, I can see that the first impulse for a life on Earth must come from the spirit side, but what about the rest? What about if I in my Conscious Mind decide to do something? Am I doing that from the spirit side or from the physical side?

Peaceful One: What is a decision to act, but a little bit of this and that mixed together to see how it works out? From whence does physical reality come from is the real question. In other words, who made the shoe store? But once the shoe store in there, you are free to go shopping and get whatever you like or even make all new and different kinds of shoes.

Joyce: Are you saying that the physical me is working with the physical ingredients and making things, but that all originated from energy, formed into physical matter?

Peaceful One: Quite so! What not to speak is just as hard a topic to form as what to say. Yes, my dear, you are here on assignment to do just what you have done and are using the resources given to you. But what say you to the fact that you are eliciting much more than others through the use of the intention for the Highest Good?

What if one person has no idea that the shoe store is even there? You at least looked where to go to find them and are telling everyone else. "I just Spoogled for a long time because I needed some shoes and see what showed up." Were you not the one to ask for the gift of explaining the true condition of the Conscious Mind and how to add to its efforts the highest and best of all minds? All who do so will have all of their needs satisfied by being offered good outcomes to choose from.

Joyce: Oh, so you are saying that the intention for the Highest Good is the critical ingredient for making all of this happen. It makes sense because the Highest Good is God and comes from God, so nothing better could be given or received. I wonder how that intention has been active in our current civilization?

Peaceful One: Why not look at ancient civilizations for their record and use them as an example of how to form a better modern society? Would you want to participate in a better rendition of the ancient Egypt experiences with the intention for the Highest Good?

Joyce: Oh yes. I love studying ancient Egypt. Why did you choose that one out of all of the other ancient civilizations?

Peaceful One: Do you not realize to whom you are speaking? Have we not made ourselves clear? We are indeed the guardians of that culture returned to do our service to the current age. We have a plan to return the Earth to peace and you came to read this record in mind, but also in ancient script, rock, and walls.

Joyce: Uh oh, I think I just crossed into another time zone. But I am interested in these ancient cultures. Yes, for sure, I would like to participate. Count me in.

Peaceful One: Consider why you did me the honor of calling me the Peaceful One to help you. It was the same for he who was once the great leader who founded Egypt and other civilizations from nothing more that what you experienced in the sunny window. Look where it took him. It will do the same for you. It always does for anyone who embarks on the journey of the soul to make peace with the intention for the Highest Good.

Joyce: Well that must mean that this man had the cooperation of the Great Oneness to count on.

Peaceful One: Where else would the intention for Highest Good take him, or you, your Reader, or anyone but to a great and peaceful society?

Joyce: That reminds me of the moment that I lifted my assumptions about what is physical and spiritual and asked about the nature of the cooperation between the two. And I want to clarify one important point. What is the difference between an action done for other than Highest Good intentions and one done solely with the intention for the Highest Good?

Peaceful One: Consider that all life comes from the spirit side and is consumed by the physical side. This is done for humans by and through their aura. Therefore, the spirit side and the human side meet rendezvous in the aura. Being separate is impossible and being together is reality. For how can a life force be denied, and people still be expected to grow and be alive? How can the light be hidden and one still see in the dark? Should one ever stop to see and hear all of the energy transmissions that are popping in and out of the human aura, it would be deafening. So let's proceed with one of the most often-told stories about time and space that Jesus told.

Joyce: Oh, good. I love these stories about Jesus. Go ahead.

Peaceful One: Which one is the truer son, the one who stays in contact supporting the father and enjoying the richness of the relationship, or the runaway son who stops at nothing to spend all that he has on foolish enterprises, and when he runs out of money, comes back to his father for more?

Joyce: That is the story of the prodigal son, but I don't see how it applies to our discussion of working with the energy of the Highest Good.

Peaceful One: With one son safely in consort with the wishes of the father, the other son is the one to be worked with. For in bringing that one home to be in enjoyment of all good things, the family is complete and the story ends. Now which son is the Conscious Mind and which is the Higher Mind? And what is the purpose of the father's intentions for both?

Joyce: This sounds like a test question but I know the answer. The prodigal son uses the Conscious Mind and finds no success, while the other son decides to cooperate with the Higher Mind and experiences the Divine with ease and comfort. The story ends with the rejoicing of the family that the son has returned and agreed to cooperate and to be happy. It sounds like the

Earth has a lot of prodigal sons using fearful Conscious Minds living here. The Father intends that all of his offspring come into joyful cooperation and live in happiness. Is that what Christ was teaching in this story?

Peaceful One: How happy would it be to be certain that the father was willing to accept back even the most ungrateful of sons and fill him up with the good things? This was the question at hand when he told this story to the people of the day, who had no confidence that a father would do such a thing. The people assumed that the father would be angry and never speak to the son again to punish him and to teach him a lesson. But Christ assured them that no, the Father loves all the same and that even the most profligate of doers of evil will be welcome when they agree to the intention of the Highest Good.

Joyce: Did Jesus use the words, Highest Good?

Peaceful One: How would the people of the day understand unless the words were in the vernacular, telling of events similar to their own family experiences? No, he called the Highest Good, my Heavenly Father's will, but it meant the same. Should the people recognize that God was a good father and submit to the gentle art of fearless regard for themselves, then they would thrive in blessedness. That was the message of the time.

Joyce: Jesus must have been a very loving teacher. At last I get the meaning of that story. It makes me realize how important it was that I agreed to avoid fear, anger, grief, and self-harm, and employed the nuclear energy of my intention for the Highest Good. I have my porcelain angel to thank for that. I pray that others will do the same and savor the joys of being in sync with the power of the Highest Good to bless us all.

Peaceful One: And with that said, the crowds crushed around Him to touch him, for His word was powerful and His touch so healing that even the hem of His cloak was regarded as sufficient to raise the dead. And so it will be with the gentle stone found by the sea, which you have purchased. It will be imbued with the energy of one dedicated to the transmission of the Highest Good. So shall all others who do the same, and so any of their personal possessions will be of value. Most certainly the stones, crystals, and rocks have a special ability to hold and enhance such energy. They will be prized as conduits of the energy of the Highest Good.

Thus we find that the deed is done and the day is drawing to a close, so let us bless this occasion with a special prayer for peace.

Let the Highest Good be done to me and through me, Divine One, that I might be blessed and be a blessing to all others, Amen.

Chapter Two: Snowballs in Hell

How can I proceed without fully understanding what has been taught to me? I have to ask for a better way to understand how vibrations and light work to create me and my life. Since I am a poet, not a scientist, I will have to use my own words and hope that scientists will later find some understanding that is of interest to them. But I do have a sense of how profound some of this information will be. For brevity and clarity, I asked for a better way to understand.

What I experienced was to have a concept dropped into my mind, expressing another view of reality. I could understand from the concept some of what was meant, and could ask questions about the rest. This was followed by a description from the Oneness that was concise, direct, and intense. It was very different from prior readings. Later I found that this information came from a group of souls called the Hathors who have been helping the civilizations of the Earth to be happy ever since the first hominid stood up on the grassy plains and said "Where am I?" The Hathors were clearly depicted in Egyptian art and the ancients consulted them often. I will give you my best understandings as well as their readings and then follow up with a dialogue so as to ease your mind with some questions and answers. I warn you that this is a very expansive view of existence with much more that will need to be explored. If you are ready, I will proceed as best I can.

To start, I asked for a description of how the Peaceful One and I interact. This required that the definition of a dimension be given because the Peaceful One is in a different dimension than I am. I researched current thought about dimensions and it is true that scientists have determined that there are dimensions outside of this physical dimension and indeed there are many of them. Current String Theory tells of vibrating strings or wheels of energy, which are the fundamental components of all matter and thus all that we experience. With that as a start, hang on to your hard hat: We're going to get a description of how the universe is constructed.

Reading: Spirals Sending Snowballs to Hell and Back

We are the Hathors and we have come to clarify and enhance an old concept, which has much more to give to the world at this time.

How awful can it sound to be calling the physical dimension Hell without an explanation of the two dimensions and how they function? Thus we must define what is a dimension.

The definition of a dimension is that of a concentrated community of souls who have gathered together to be of service and to experience each other and their creations. They are physical only to the extent that the consensual belief systems of the residents have crystallized or condensed into various forms as needed for the continuation of the community or dimension. A dimension is a personal thing, not a destination or a place. Some dimensions are shimmering degrees of latitude formed in the mind of a man in search of himself. Others are far reaches of inner space where compassion or contentment reign as the law of the community, as is often encountered by meditators. In the case of the physical dimension, much crystallization of thought has occurred so that vast numbers of physical objects have formed by design and will continue to do so. This Earthly dimension is a unique opportunity to experience life in a much more slow, dense, but solid way than the other dimensions. For our purposes, we will discuss this physical dimension, whose color vibration is green (which we jokingly call Hell), and the next dimension called the Blue or Etheric Dimension in which we reside and from which human souls came and to which they will return. It is a place of peace and so the price of admission is a peaceful mind.

As we have implied, there is a way to enter and exit each dimension. It is more by application with a selected trajectory in mind and with the full support of the community of departure as well as the one to which one is headed. There are a minimum of 3,500 dimensions that have controlled entry and exit points within the reach of your physical dimension of time and space. Each of these communities is more like a bacteria colony in a glass culture dish. Hosts of mini communities exist within each dimension, so guidance committees are available to assist with the departure from one and the search for the next. The guides arrange for your entrance and exit. Then there is a reception committee prepared to help make the adjustments to the new environment. It is not necessary to leave the physical body or to use mechanical vehicles to enter and exit these dimensions for they are spiritual/mental communities.

Within each colony there are those whose responsibility it is to oversee and to organize the thought processes to be in alignment with the charter of the community. There are those of the green thumb interest who study and create plants, sharing complete knowledge of their culture and use. And they rely upon others to be the metals committee who cast metal knowledge, ready to share that technology, etc. All is kept in order without constraining the free will of a soul to pass through or to stay for a while. Thus it is within each nation of an intentional community that there are members of guilds or trades, all of whom assist anyone who inquires when needed and withdraw when not needed.

Within each dimension, there is a Great Caretaker who has charge of communication between the dimensions and those within each. In this current physical dimension, the Great Caretaker is the Christ Consciousness. It is with the assistance of the Christ Consciousness that communication back and forth has been supplied with many easy opportunities for mutual help. With this, there is the need to be given the location or address of the opening to communication as well as the password. This is essentially what Christ did after his supposed death when he said that he left to prepare places within his father's mansion for his followers. With that accomplished, modern man could more easily access the dominions of grace in the Blue Dimension. The address of the Blue Dimension is the closest to the physical and is where the intention for the Highest Good or Benign Oneness resides. The password is Peace.

Once one has made one's own access often enough to the Blue Dimension that it is easy and convenient, there is no limit to the assistance that can be given to and from each other as long as it is for grace.

This wanderlust between the two dimensions is no chance encounter, however, for it must be applied for by the soul and supported by the Great Oneness before a lifetime even begins. At this point, all that needs to be in alignment is set in motion to be played out during the lifetime. Once the openings to the desired dimensions are familiar, there are many more that will be made available just for the asking.

The one who opens to a dimension must be a good questioner and asker of grace as well as a good listener and documentarian. After that, there are those of the librarian nature who will document, research and verify the passages to and fro for generations to respect and follow. Such documentation was done in ancient times and depicted on the temple and tomb walls in Egypt. They called the physical world the underworld or Land of the Minds Dead to the Other Dimensions and the Blue Dimension the sky world or afterlife. Their journey was to resurrect themselves from the physical or Conscious Mind to the Blue or Higher Mind. Just look at the ceilings painted royal blue with gold stars. Those stars are us, by the way. We are the gold stars in the Blue Dimension. In other ceilings we are standing around indicating our place in the Great Oneness. It is with this old relationship and common knowledge in mind, that we are making the journey from the Blue Dimension back to you, in order to give these readings. The password we used to reach you is Oneness.

Since each dimension is a colony of colonies, there is the interaction between them to consider, for they are good neighbors and fond friends from different places of mind. Once the Blue Dimension has been explored, there will be no need to determine from whence grace comes, for so much energy of life is poured from the Blue to the physical dimension as to be a complex interchange of umbilical cords, each a spiral tube of light. These are the vibrating strings that theorists are beginning to understand. Thus it can safely be said that not one thing happens upon the physical plane without help and support from the Blue.

That is why the Blue Dimension is the first and easiest to explore. In fact, exploring it is as close as one's own skin. If you would take an energetic photo of the physical body through which the soul is participating in a lifetime, you would see a human body within an energy womb. Look once again at the front cover of this book. You will see the bone and muscle of a body within its skin surrounded by a layered set of lights each containing the resources, plans, and abilities needed to support and give life a chance to express itself as is the soul's intention. This is what is known as the Human Aura. As connecting points between the aura and the body, there is the system of spiral cords called chakras or wheels of life energy. These are constantly in motion either one way or the other (clockwise or counterclockwise) to assist the life plan.

However, it is not correct to call it an automatic function, rather it is an intended attention to every detail of your existence from us in the Blue Dimension guided by the soul whom Joyce calls The Peaceful One. The Peaceful One is in charge of that particular lifetime. In fact, the layer of bright blue light surrounding the skin is your part of the Blue Dimension that delivers all of the resources that you need to complete your life plan. Life, therefore, is a personal gift from one being of light to one in another dimension and it is the responsibility of the giver to establish and maintain the entrance and exit between the dimensions. In fact, the Blue Dimension Giver delivers life in orbs of light that dance around in the air, to be captured by the receiving chakras in need of a particular gift of energy. One need only extend one's spiral tube of need to capture all that is needed.

Thus there is a Human, the observer, who comes into physical existence with a Conscious Mind to use, not knowing from whence it came and with no idea of what to do or where to go. However brief a life might be, there is always a purpose that produces Highest Good, for that is all that both dimensions can access, express, produce, or replicate. With this in mind, there is the need to be alert to the many comings and goings of thoughts, emotions, memories, and energy transfers within the human aura, for they are all signs of the kind of life that is unfolding.

If one has the mental facility to be able to form a contact with one's own soul and its group, there is the wonderful privilege to be taught by willing cooperation, how to accomplish the Highest Good, not by the spoonful, but by the bucketful. Thus, Joyce has dubbed her soul, The Peaceful One, and none other will reply unless requested. As her lifetime is designed to be an expression of the Opener of Channels in assistance with the work of the Christ Consciousness, she often hears from Him as well. His residence is the Dimension of the Contented Ones, which is the color of pearly white with blue accents and the password is Contentment. One must pass through the Blue Dimension to get to the Contented Dimension and so forth to others, often showing a blend of the colors of each.

With this understood, there is the need to be certain of the nature of the human aura and this is the main concern of this book. Once one sees oneself as an energetic body of light, one will never make the mistake of thinking that one is alone or lost or in fear of anything. Once that is sure, then there is the life plan to understand and accomplish. Indeed, it is one and the same thing to be in love with oneself, the same as another, since all are members of one colony of love, in love with all others and firmly attached to the great colony Giver of Grace: God, the Creator. Therefore, all life plans have something to do with the river of life giving orbs that flows from God through all of the great colonies, even into the physical one of time and space.

And so we finally understand that the snowballs sent to Hell are the orbs of light that are sent from the Blue Dimension, where nothing but peace exists, to the Physical Dimension where fear can exist as the living Hell of doubt. One might be separated from the river of life simply because one cannot remember where one came from, why one is here, and what one is to do while here. Once the doubt is eliminated by a conscious choice to do so, called faith, then the revelations begin. The story is pieced together and more help than the Conscious Mind can ever conceive is given.

The process by which life is given is to be understood through the study of the Human Aura. No science experiment in space is needed to prove the existence of other dimensions: Simply open one's heart, made too small by suspicion and greed, to be accepting of the grace of life that is swimming all around one. Thus we find that light theory seen as a collage of different kinds of tiny orbs that are projected through space from the sun to bless the Earth and its inhabitants must be discussed next.

For light theory to be understood, it is necessary to follow the line of thought that Einstein offered, that light travels in a path at a prescribed speed in all directions and does not end, even though it can be bent, reflected or refracted to display its components. As the physical manifestation of God's love, light never stops. When bending or reflection of light occurs, there is the release of much energy of various kinds. When light flows through a crystalline form at a certain angle, it is refracted and its components displayed in different colors and wavelengths. Thus the refraction of light through the Earth's atmosphere, containing tiny droplets of water, is largely responsible for life on Earth. There are color ranges within light – only partially seen in rainbows – that foster certain types of life forms. As the atmosphere swirls, curves and bends around the Earth, it forms a giant lens of refraction, which allows a variety of life forms because much that is destructive to this type of life is returned to space. Thus, that which is benign to earth is allowed in and all else prohibited. The miracle of light and life are clearly one.

Without light, life would not occur. This is not just because food would not grow, but because the energy orbs created by sunlight, offering all manner of gifts for life, would not be floating around looking for a place to be used. Indeed, the human aura is such an orb. It is an orb so concentrated with the intention for a particular human life that it congealed into bone and muscle. However it might seem, the human body draws life energy not only from food and oxygen, but also from the orb/aura that surrounds it. Indeed the Beings of Light intending to be humans brought with them the Blue Light energy to access their Blue Dimension partners so as to receive the many gifts of grace that they provide moment by moment.

For all life on the physical dimension is transmitted through orbs of light traveling at great speed. When orbs are reflected or refracted, they propagate into many different varieties each with their own gift to create life. And so the sun is the local transmitter of the original orb system from the Blue Dimension as its thermonuclear reaction instantly transfers energy between the dimensions. The orbs of light from the sun are refracted through water droplets in the environment when they come to the Earth. This is the reason for a blue sky. It illustrates just how close the Earth is to the blue dimension. If one would find the Egyptian wall carving showing the sun disk with rays of light ending in little hands offering gifts, one would see that they understood this concept very well.

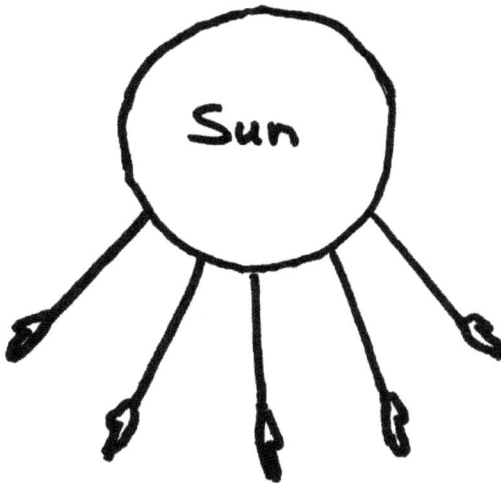

Drawing 1: Gifts of Sunlight

With this in mind, it is necessary to discuss how life flies in the face of destruction by multiplying itself over and over, both in the same form improved, as well as entirely new forms. For when light is refracted, it has a multiplying effect of spraying many more particles of grace into the space of Earth than if it were directly received from the sun. As one sees from space, there is not the beauty of multicolored light anywhere else than on the planets, stars, and asteroids with atmospheres, however slight, even those composed of dust or smoke, which multiply the possibilities for life.

The fact of refracted light being the precious source of life on Earth was depicted in the ancient Egyptian world as the flail that starts as one braided pole, but ends in the braids being undone into many strands of differing beauty and grace. Thus we end this part of the book with the prayer of the Egyptian queen who found herself in the underworld of Conscious Mind too long, and wished to exit to the light, and so she sang the song of all Egyptian Pharaohs: "I make my way to the light and make peace to be my entrance and exit. Make peace be mine."

+

With that we will pause so you can also get a breath of fresh air and a walk in the sunshine. So much that has been presented here is so obvious, you will come to see that everything is a vibrating circle of light; and that the exchange of orbs of light is the very existence of life, caught in the act of giving and receiving energetic resources, multiplying and prospering them. From these resources, each person creates more and more that is unique and individual from their own perspective. It sound like fun to be alive, don't you think?

+

Dialogue

After a walk, some fresh air, lunch, and a nap, my mind is still turning over this whole thing. Yes, it sounds simple and obvious that we are all a huge community connected to our great Source of Life. The Long Story, as told in Book 2, said that we are souls created to be loved and to give love, so we are in different dimensions or thought worlds doing that in great variety and purpose. And it would make sense that we would want to help each other and to communicate freely. But what are these spirals and what do they have to do with the human aura? What is this about light theory? I need a dialogue to help me with this.

Joyce: First of all, thanks for the definition of a dimension. I guess I thought it was someplace out in space where things were very weird and I certainly didn't want to go there. But from your description, it's really like a website where people who have a common interest log in, discuss their topics, and give help to each other. It might also be compared to a university where there are departments of special interest, like history or engineering. People interested in those topics go there to meet, discuss, and learn. Some stay a long time and others a short time.

Now, let me follow that analogy and ask a question. Do Beings of Light reside in a dimension but are free to come and go?

Peaceful One: How good would a webmaster be without being able to answer that question? The Christ Consciousness would say that He resides in His own dimension in thought, but that his energy form travels wherever it wants to in the form of an orb. Now you will have to ask me the next question. What is an orb?

Joyce: Just what I was thinking! Yes, go ahead.

Peaceful One: An orb is an energy vortex much like a dust devil or tornado carrying within it objects. But much like a snowball that has congealed into ice and gotten firm or solidified, it can also then change form under certain conditions. Think of a frozen snowball that can melt and be water, then warm and turn into mist or steam. It will turn into clouds then reform into smaller balls, like hail, or snow or even into something bigger, like an iceberg. Where does an orb get this intention to change and to be somewhere in one form and then leave? Why, of course, from the intentional source of its existence: its source, the Soul, residing in one dimension or another.

Joyce: I like the analogy of the snowball melting and changing forms into hail, snow, or even mist. That makes sense, and I think that you are saying that an orb is a bit of life energy formed under certain conditions to serve the intention for the Highest Good. Coming from another dimension, an orb is a gift of one's own energy as a being in one dimension to come and go in another. We get to be another version of ourselves in this dimension in order to experience something of interest. Am I right?

Peaceful One: What do you think that you are, my dearest and sweetest? You are a body and mind living in an orb sent to the physical dimension to experience life there, while being directed and supported by me/yourself in the Blue Dimension. Would that you would be made aware that you are not unconnected or left to your own devices. You are intimately connected to me and to all who interact with me. I think of you as an intentional toe that I stuck in the sand on the beach of physical reality to feel its coolness, and when I am done, I will withdraw it and go on to another place to experience another beach. The only difference is that you have a consciousness of your own and can make choices to experience what you want and I *have* to come along. Better to say that you are my child out exploring in the woods and I have to come along to take care of you, because you are me and I love you and I sent you there for a purpose. We both want it to be a success.

Joyce: So you are my parent and caretaker as well as best friend.

Peaceful One: All of that and more.

Joyce: I remember Jesus saying that: "I and the Father are one." That takes on a new meaning now. So you are going to say that I am an orb of you and that you send orbs of life energy to me to keep me alive and prospering here, right? But actually we are one being in two different forms. How can I say such a thing? But actually, I *think* that I understand it. The key is to get rid of the idea of separation and see these orbs as flows of energy, not individuals. I am thinking of a tornado that can touch down to earth for an instant and then be drawn back up into the clouds the next.

Peaceful One: Congratulation, you have taken a mighty step in the right direction. And all will proceed nicely if only you will accept all of the orbs as a gift of life, which are balls of light of various colors and qualities, which I send you. Some you like and some you dislike. But I sent them all to you as gifts of grace. If you do not take all of them as grace, then we will miss our mark.

Joyce: What are you referring, to that I do not accept?

Peaceful One: How about the one who told you that you are stubborn and you took offense, when I only wanted to compliment you on standing strong in fearlessness?

Joyce: I remember. It was someone trying to be helpful, but I refused the help. That one was an orb?

Peaceful One: A person living within an orb who responded to my message and gave it to you loud and clear.

Joyce: That's funny. You got your message to me through another person who was listening to you through his aura. I can see that we are all orbs of light that solidified into bone and muscle, still connected to our parents in the Blue Dimension, who are whispering in our minds: "Do this, say this." It's a light conspiracy!

Peaceful One: Well, I wouldn't go that far and say that all who love an orb are also in love with the creator of the orb, would you? And if both orbs have love for each other then they can generate many more orbs and so become parents themselves. Surely that is not too far out to accept, do you think?

Joyce: Well, as long as you are that far out there tell me more about light transmission through space, particularly light bouncing off of the moon and being filtered through the atmosphere to the surface of the Earth. After all, we started this book talking about moonlight.

Peaceful One: Would that you know that one begets the other as in any family. Once an orb of light passes through space and reaches the moon, it is transformed by the moon's dust and sent in a new direction, such as to the Earth. There it is transformed once again as it passes through the atmosphere, which is filled with dust and water vapor. In the atmosphere of Earth, it passes through one more transformation, which gives it its typical blue color. The light coming to Earth is filtered of all other colors except those related to the Blue Dimension so that all who have come from that dimension can live there in peace.

Once that is accomplished, there is yet another filtering of the gift of life. The human consciousness can accept or block the Cosmic Code of the Highest Good, which takes place within the human consciousness. This is done in the atmosphere of the human aura where thoughts and feelings are held. If the thoughts and feelings are of peace, then all is right and peace reigns supreme within that body/mind. If not, then not, and fear is free to reside and to grow in that one's consciousness, even to the point of being seen as personified evil.

Some indeed agree to live as an evil one and to test out their mental powers to overcome the peaceful ones who, of course, ignore the challenge and just come straight to the truth, asking for more orbs of peace to be sent so as to make all happy and serene. Indeed, if one or two or even three, as we are doing in this reading, decide to put the Fearful One back in its place and invite the peaceful beings of the Blue Dimension in, then fear leaves and peace returns.

And so we come to the premise of this book, that although there has been mass misery of great proportions abounding on the Earth, there is no need for it to continue. Once it is known that the simple choice to free oneself from fear and to accept all experiences in the light of the intention for the Highest Good, then all *will* be light and no evil *can* exist, and thus it is so.

Joyce: You just said a mouthful. So let me chew on it for a while. I'm getting a clearer picture that the Earth's atmosphere and the human aura are much the same and do similar things. That's a strange thought, but a good one. After I swallow all of this, we can go on with a much deeper question: If we are all orbs and orbs are floating around everywhere, what is the energy source that propels and maintains them?

Peaceful One: Could it be that the personal intention to create constantly calls in and collects energy to fill the needs of creation? Could it be that all are fed by the original gift of life that came from God and still comes? Could it be that intention is the basis of all created existence? Is it intention that organizes and directs the energy of light to create beautiful experiences? Could it be that the original intention was the Highest Good and all similar intentions get to help themselves to the same vast resources of light? What if someone wanted to create evil; wouldn't that also have to work for the good through karma, otherwise it would have no energy to use? Oh, what a mystery we have unearthed and brought to the light. Need I say more?

Joyce: Since I cannot answer a single one of these questions because they are self-evident, I call a truce. Let's take a break. I need some chocolate.

Chapter Three:
A Vibrational Universe of Spirals

Joyce: Yum. Nothing calms me down like chocolate. After some time thinking about what I just learned, I realized that I was letting go of how I was viewing myself as human. Before, I saw myself as an independent bipedal mass of bone, muscle, blood, and nerves walking around, pretty much disconnected from all others, and doing whatever I wanted or could do. I thought that I was a stand-alone unit. After I do what I want for a long time, I deteriorate and die and that is that, for one lifetime. But now, I'm thinking that I am an eternal consumer of light energy constantly construct-ing and reconstructing experiences, which include new bodies to live in. So I created my body and I created chocolate and I created the experience of eating it. This is getting very interesting. By the way, I think I enjoy the idea of being the Divine Chocolatier. I think that I shall have dark chocolate and chip it up to be made into confections of all different kinds. If it worked for God, it works for me!

I'd be curious to see how the Peaceful One and the Hathors see humans.

The Perspective of the Hathors

I'd like to introduce you to your human experience from the point of view of spirit living in the Blue Dimension. Spirit sees you as a bubble of light, vibrating with your life energy, your thoughts, and your emotions. The bubble is the human aura and the physical body lives within it. This bubble of light is contained within a larger bubble of light along with many other bubbles just like yours for as far as you can imagine. You are part of a very large organism. You might look at the front and back cover to get a visual image of this.

These bubbles are really swirling vortexes of energy formed by the intention to create them. They were originated by the Great Creator and kept in existence by the Beings of Light in the Blue Dimension. The intention of the Creator began like a bubble machine, shooting out live rivers of orbs. You might think of wind blowing in a direction that blows bubbles in the same direction, but this is not exactly how it looks. All energy flows in spirals, so these bubbles look like they are coming out of coiled springs and thus they travel in spiraling trajectories.

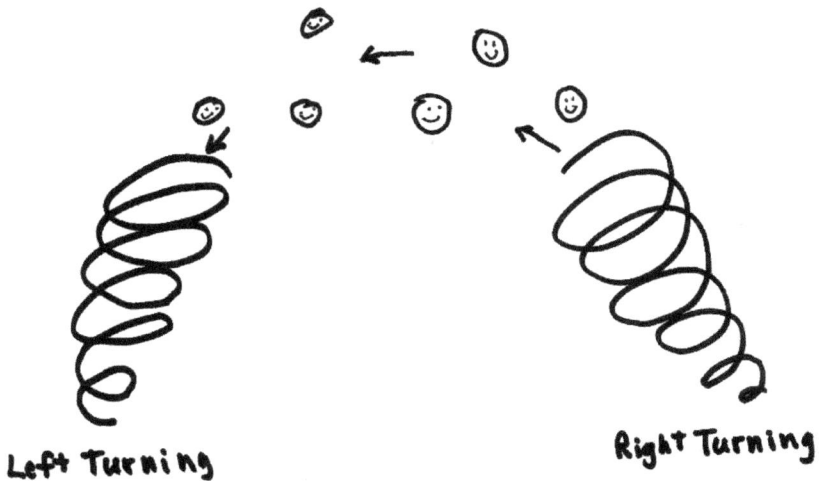

Left Turning   Right Turning

Drawing 2: Spirals and Orbs

Since the universe is a spiral one, you might also think of God's intention as a non-destructive tornado. These are the spirals or vortexes that give life and they have certain characteristics. They constantly open and close to give and receive life force orbs in unlimited vibrational patterns and frequencies which create the many different forms of life in each dimension. Many religions talk about the wind or the breath of God moving over the waters to create life. Sometimes it is called the singing of the stars because sound travels the same way, in spirals. These are ways to express that God moves in vibrational patterns and these patterns are so diverse and powerful that an intention in one dimension can create physical matter in another dimension. Thus you, as a human body, are living within a bubble of light connected by spiral vortexes to the organism of all others and thereby to God.

The behavior of these vortexes or spirals is very flexible. Vortexes are circular in nature. They hum and vibrate in very precise patterns. The patterns are very elaborate with many layers of different functions and forms. One vortex pattern can create an ant and another an elephant, but they are all linked together in an organized pattern of giving and receiving energy – essentially a relationship community. The vortexes reach out from one to another, giving and receiving energy as well as creating channels of communication.

The vortexes can open wide or narrow down. They can stretch through many dimensions or retract to connect just two cells from the retina of your eye to a single nerve cell in the brain. Some can spin in two directions. On the outside, they spin clockwise and, on the inside, counter-clockwise creating movement to and from, like a hub cap that goes forward with the turning of the wheel, but an inside part spins backwards. An orb can attach to one being or location to another by will or need, and then let go and attach somewhere else. They can produce smaller orbs of light energy to spit out and give to another vortex or they can receive an orb from another.

With these vortexes in place, the whole collage as viewed from spirit space, appears to be a wall of shimmering energy wheels which curl and fold within each other, all alive and registering the essential directive to reproduce their version of the Divine. These structures are like petals of a rose or better yet a sea fan coral that waves in the currents of life. They are all interconnected and share the same life force.

There are bee-like forces, which attend to their every need. First there are the pollinators of sound, which can travel from one petal to another to nourish and communicate with all. Sound carries the Presence of God in vibrational form and travels everywhere that it can. It has tone, melody, rhythm, and harmony. The player of the music for the Earth Dimension, Christ Consciousness, is the Master of this part of the universe, who sees to it that there are none who go amiss or lives without the constant infusion of the grace of God. This grace is sent in the form of vibrations like music, organized by theme, melody, harmony and rhythm. This music can be heard from space, for it proceeds from the vibrations of the Earth and emanates in radiant circles, accelerating rather than losing energy. It is joined by the great symphonic voices of all who dwell on other planets and in other spaces. It is with this harmonic frequency of the music of the spheres, that the Great Pyramid was tuned so that it, sitting at the center of the continental mass of the Earth, could amass as much Earth energy as needed to effect the current changes toward peace for life on Earth.

The Dialogue Continues

Joyce: Put on the brakes here for a minute! This is a lot for me to understand. I was watching a DVD on String Theory, as the current astrophysicists see it, and they said that they have mathematically proven that there are shimmering strands or circles of energy, which vibrate and form everything. Is that what you are talking about when you say vortexes?

Peaceful One: No matter that the string is a theory and we are the vortex providers, but yes, such matters are currently being better understood. Astrophysicists have come to believe that there are membranes of strings that interconnect. They think that these membranes are simultaneous dimensions and that the connections are wormholes between the dimensions. They are not perfectly correct, but acceptance of these very challenging ideas is proceeding nicely.

Let us take a current string idea and advance it even more. Suppose that we are the guides to the string theorists whispering these ideas directly into their minds and they are open to hearing us because they gave up their Newtonian and Einstein-based beliefs. What would you say to that?

Joyce: I'd say that they are channeling like I do, but are not aware of it. You must be giving away a lot of secrets these days.

Peaceful One: How could one union of intent and purpose keep secrets from each other? They want to find the truth that explains everything and we are in the business of offering them, as much as they can understand, then give them more.

Joyce: Yes, it is a grand goal and they are expending a lot of effort, paper, and pencil on their equations. May they experience the Highest Good and none else. They also mention the forces of the universe. They list then as gravity, electromagnetism, and the strong and the weak atomic forces. I take it that you would include sound as a force.

Peaceful One: Most certainly, but how weak or strong would we be if we did not mention that the force of gravity is not clearly understood. If you don't mind, we will proceed with that discussion.

Joyce: Be my guest, or rather I am your guest in a battle of the blackboards of science theory. If you don't mind, I'll sit in the back of the class and just listen.

+

Hathors: The term gravity was best described by Einstein as a dimple in a fabric that holds a body in position. We see it as an intention that holds all in virtual motion, shimmering in tune with the Divine and thus holding all in place. So think of gravity not as a weight-giving force, but as a holding-in-place force. This is accomplished by the multiple layers of intentions, of which we will speak when we discuss the human aura. These layers of intentions interact in harmony to create and to hold in position a physical object in a time and a place until the experience is completed. Thus the solar system has an aura much like the Earth's magnetic field and each being upon it. Each planet has a position in the solar system aura and is held in place by its vortex within which it spins. Thus it is called gravity.

Although it is the weakest of the forces, gravity is the greatest proponent of life on Earth. Without gravity, nothing would function as it should and therefore life, as you know it, would vanish. No rain would fall from the sky. Rocks, dust and water would float around everywhere. Cold water would not sink to the bottom of the ocean, creating the rotational flow of ocean currents that control the temperature of the Earth. There would be no deposits of salts and minerals, which turn to dust and are blown around the world to fertilize plant growth in distant forests. There would be no churning of lava within the Earth, which causes the movement of the continental plates, thus recycling and releasing minerals necessary for life. It is all done by intention, supplied through the activity of vortexes and orbs.

Gravity is further described as being caused by the clockwise turning of the Earth and its liquid core. As it turns, it draws inward the grace of the light emanations from the sun. Together, light and gravity cause weather and the stabilization of the air and ionosphere, which makes life possible. Particles rubbing together in weather patterns cause lightening which rebalances the electromagnetic forces around the Earth. Thus gravity is the cause for the organization of things to be in place where place is an issue such as it is on Earth. Remembering that gravity is a gift of an intentional orb with a planet inside gives you some idea of the loving presence which

56

keeps earth so beautiful. It represents a great gift, don't you think?

This organization took place when God, in the midst of the storm of chaos said: "Quiet down and be one and the same with the Highest Good as was designed." Those who disturbed the environment of the Earth with their fearful thinking had failed to ascertain how and why such order could be had, but it was. Thus they came to their senses and began to experience lives of more order. And so it will come to pass, once again, that the order of the Highest Good will be called forth to stabilize and order the forces of the Earth once again for the good of all. In short, the intention for the Highest Good is the gravity of peaceful living.

With this understanding intact, there is yet another force to behold that has yet to be discussed as to its use: base strength verses acid strength expressed as PH. These twin, but opposite, poles of interaction between these same but opposite forces form the balance of reactivity and resistance. Together, in balance, they create a condition of wholeness and health. Without this balance, all would be out of balance and the mixture of forces would fall into disrepair. Therefore, there are some in the community of life who are reactors of the highest level. Some are reactors at the medium, balanced level and some are reactors with the lowest reactivity and have the most resistance. The forces of reactivity and resistance are opposite and balancing and were put into place at the beginning of chemical, atomic, and emotional life on Earth. Without this dynamic of reactivity and resistance balancing these two kinds of strength, no life could be maintained. They are the inhalation and exhalation of the Divine breath

57

of life. They reflect the Divine trait of giving and receiving love. As was stated at the beginning of this book, those in most need are most reactive to help and those in least need are not so. Thus the founding principle of all peaceful relations is to find first the most needy or reactive and fill the need with resources. When all reactivity is satisfied, there is joyfulness, followed by more need and more filling.

₊

Joyce: Are you amazed, Dear Reader, at what meticulously coordinated natural systems were set in benign order during the design of the universe? It is the hand of a good Creator with a desire to create a place of peace and happiness. All of these systems have been studied and documented by humans, both on the planetary scale as seen from satellites in space, as well as on the microscopic scale in test tubes. Even obscure scientists are inspired to come forth to make DVD's to illustrate that life is so complex and intelligent that it is hard to see how we *cannot* be at peace. Only the fears of our Conscious Minds could cause any of this to go astray.

Peaceful One: What a grand statement of intent the natural systems of the planet present. Would that a God, so profoundly loving and benign, be given the due respect of a communication of appreciation and gratitude for it was not always this way. As alluded to in the Bible, there once was much chaos on this planet as on others, with conditions prohibitive of life. What was the voice that called chaos to order? Was it Christ Consciousness who had charge of this dimension and whose name was essentially **Peace**? He did it in complete cooperation with God, who created all manner of souls to be in communication in all dimensions as they experience life. We urge you to continue on in peace, for each ounce of peace is precious. It contributes further to the balance of these great forces of nature and assures that all will continue as planned.

Now let us introduce to you another group of entities that wish to tell you a story of peace. You may call them The Storytellers. They have entertained and educated their earth partners about these truths for a very long time.

The Storytellers: We delight to return to this time and place and to enjoy an alternative way that this information may be transmitted, for not all are scientists. Being that we have told this story to the Greek philosophers long ago, but it was not recorded for history, it gives us great pleasure to repeat it to you now.

Joyce: We all love to hear a good story.

Storytellers: Once there was a little star whose vast awareness started to focus on a desire to play a game. And so the little star consulted its mother and father star to ask for assistance as to where to go to play the game. The little star was directed to the Earth plane, which was painted in the color green. Because the little star was a blue star, it had to change its own color to be green to match the play yard where it was going and thus it was so.

As the little star entered into the play yard, there were other little stars there as well, all green. They had been playing there for a long time and had established the rules of the play to be mean to each other. The new little star began to play and was jostled around, but learned a few of the moves seeking to enjoy such a strange place where one could possibly be harmed. However, after a time, the little star began to forget that he was originally a blue star and he came from a place where the rules were gentle kindness. So the little star became like the others and played and played, building great teams in conflict with each other.

One day, the little star had a faint memory of something not being right and settled down on a grassy hill to ponder the thought. He noted that many of the fallen players were injured and could not play any more and that indeed he could suffer the same fate. And so he determined to find a better way to play so that all could continue in fun.

With this in mind, he changed the rules wherever he played and not a one of the other players liked it. They even kicked him off of their team leaving him all alone. So the little star pleaded with his parent stars to come and help him to change the way that the game was being played and they did. They reminded him of another experience that he had in the Nebula system where he made a change in the play and it caused the planets to cool and to form an atmosphere in which life could continue. He had called it Peace.

Thus, he tried to find a way to restore this planet to peace but, being alone, he had a difficult time of it. Then his parent stars reminded him that he had brothers and sisters who had helped him in other places who would return for the same duty, if he called them. Thus he called and they responded by leaving their blue home behind and becoming green players. Together they founded a new society in a remote place where no one cared to come.

As they prospered, other blue ones came and soon they were the most admired society on the planet and they began to teach the other green players the new rules of play. It worked for a very long time, but then the meanies came back in great numbers and reordered their recruits in the mean ways. Time and time again, the comings and goings of the blue were marked by the awareness of the value of the peaceful ways.

Eventually, there were enough who liked being treated in a gentle and kind way that one by one, the injured players came to be healed and blessed. Gradually they all came to the realization that the mean rules helped no one and agreed to participate in playing the kind and gentle rules until there was no one left willing to play by the mean rules.

Yet, something was missing and that was the blue color that was their origin. And so they asked around and found that there was a great fountain of many colors that flowed throughout the underground tunnels and they went there to participate in some color play. And in playing in other colors, they found themselves to be transformers into any color. With that thought, they become not just green ones, or blue ones, but many colored ones and with that the players asked to go to other playgrounds to see what it was like to play in all of the colors.

When the little star returned to its parents, they were proud of him because he had played the greatest game of all and done what stars do so well, express God's love.

Joyce: What a cute story! I get that you are saying that once we discover all of the other dimensions, we will have discovered that we are ones who can play anywhere, and have done so for a very long time. Hummm. So the point of all of this Earth experience is to find out that we are little stars in a galaxy of stars and we can explore it all in perfect peace. We can even become different colors and live in and communicate with many different dimensions. I think that this is what this book is all about.

In fact the first two books of this series could be summarized as: "Hello, Green Dimension, this the Blue calling. Can you hear us? Apparently, not very well. Turn down the volume of fear and dial in The Peace Channel and the static will clear. There, that's better. Now, let's talk."

Reading on Dimensions

The next dimension to the physical dimension is called the Blue Dimension for it has the signature of that color. It is within this dimension that we who are called the Great Oneness reside and give our assistance. Without it, there are none who can succeed in the Earth Dimension to understand what is about to happen. For in addition to you, Dear Reader, there are many who have been accessing this dimension without much success. At last there is one who has done her duty to alert all as to how to make this connection perfectly understandable. As soon as one has a comfortable and consistent door open to the next neighborhood; there are indeed more to explore, each having its attribute needed for admittance and acceptance of its gifts. With each introduction into the Blue Dimension, there is the need to be at peace, plus a few other infusions of specific energy patterns for each dimension. All intention is a vibration in a spiral form such as a cello playing a melody over several vibrating strings joins tones into one mellow one. The more who vibrate with the same hum, the easier it is for all to enter and to leave dimensions. Peace is a harmonious symphony.

+

Joyce: This goes back to my DVD on string theory. It was hard to understand, because the scientists of astrophysics were discussing what their formulas and equations were showing. They talked about shimmering walls of round energy strands. When you describe it as my personal experience of opening to channel, which I now see as a wormhole to the Blue Dimension, then it is easy for me to see, because I have experienced it. Better yet, you describe the openings between dimensions as tubules, instead of saying wormholes or even channels. I think that dimensional tubing would be an appropriate term, for it is a thrill ride like tubing down a river. It is complete with a few rapids followed by peaceful floating, but all in a good direction.

Drawing 3: Tubing Down the River

Peaceful One: Well then, so be it. So few have come with their inner tubes of faith in the Highest Good fully inflated, plunked them in the river, and shoved off from the bank, that it's a virtually unknown sport. We have gone to great trouble to be so explicit so that you are now able to teach it to others. As the pioneer tuber, you may have the right to establish the verbiage of travel so to speak.

Joyce: Thanks, I'll enjoy that, but let's press on with the question of: "How do I do that?" Can these dimensions be seen or detected by instruments? I'm sure that the scientists would like to know.

Peaceful One: There you go again taking into consideration the good of all beings, including the ones who are so precise as to need proof so that all can see and believe. Thus we have provided the necessary funds for much more research and when it is found to be nothing but a mental reality of intention formed a long time ago in a far away place, they will be stymied as to how to depict such mental realities as the components of a physical one. Therefore, we must state that it is not physical, but it *is* energetic. With that we will press onward, talking about vibration and how physical reality is hard or soft, reactive or resistant, depending on the nature of the atomic structure, which is of course, a set of motions, set in place by the will of the Creator of all forces.

Joyce: I never thought that I'd be taking such a long journey into the nature of the universe. By the time I get done with this book, I will have an advanced degree in Dimensional Tubing. But before I go further, I think that I will ask about a force that has great economic importance to our planet: electricity. What can you give me on that topic? Go easy, I'm still getting my feet on the ground in this classroom and I've worn down my pencil to a stub.

Perspective of the Hathors

A force gives vibration a direction or purpose. It is essentially an intention. The forces of light, sound, resistance, and reactivity have been introduced in their true nature, so let us proceed with yet another basic force.

We now need the definition of electromagnetism, as this force is also universal in nature and can function in all dimensions. In fact, it powers most of the machinery of the Green and Blue dimensions and shall continue to do so for quite some time. Although electromagnetism is not fully understood by scientists today, it should be noted that none of the ancient electricians were electrocuted; therefore natural electromagnetism is a gentle and benign force of nature, which also can be collected and distributed in complete peace.

Therefore, we advance the understanding of electromagnetism to call it the direction-giver of electrons, giving energy from one to the other in the determined direction. It is essentially an aura that draws electrons in a given direction and not the other. The electrons are giving orbs of energy from one to the other atom in a specified direction. Electrons give an impulse or wave of pressure called electricity in either of two directions, either right turning or left turning. One is the, so-called, heavy force which, inhibits change or tends to still motion, influencing it to come to rest (more resistance and less acceleration) using the right-turning direction. The other force that excites and accelerates is called the weak force and it causes electricity to increase until it flows as power to be applied for the doing of work (more acceleration and less resistance) using the left-turning direction. Therefore, there is the understanding that the electrons are not particles as seen under electron microscopes, but rather the weak or strong forces of directional turning which cause an atom to be solid and resistant, or soft and pliable. A wire wrapped in a right-turning direction around a charged bar of metal does not result in electricity flowing, but a wire wrapped in the left-turning direction does. The result of electromagnetism established around a metal bar is electricity, indeed a powerful force, but realize that it will not flow without electromagnetism to give it the direction of flow that is the Highest Good.

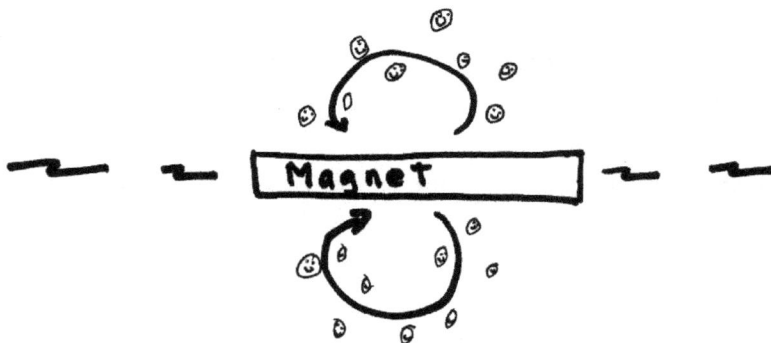

Drawing 4: Electromagnetism and Electricity

That brings us to the magnetic fields of the Earth, which do the same thing. The electromagnetic fields of the Earth, seen as the aura borealis, direct orbs sent from the sun to flow in a direction for a purpose. There are the polar flows created by rotation and the east to west flows created by the energy pulses of the warming sun. These directional flows of electromagnetism move through the atmosphere, the water, the ground and magma. They are all in harmony due to their original direction or intention to do the Highest Good to protect a planet of peaceful life.

The same is true of the human aura. There is an electromagnetic field around every human, which directs the orbs of energy for the good of the body. This magnetic field or field of light known as the human aura gives definition to the shape and nature of the physical being living there, and without it, the physical body would cease to be able to live at all.

It is a good thing that all of the electromagnetic forces are all benign and organized to produce the Highest Good. It is a good thing that living in the strong electromagnetic field of the Earth greatly enhances the electromagnetic field of a human body, because they are in complete compliance with the same intention. It is a good thing that a human who has a strong electromagnetic field can share that with another who has a weak or sick one. Just ask Christ who healed people simply by showing up and sharing his field of light. Guess why Christ and the saints spent a lot of time in secluded natural places like caves and mountains where the Earth's electromagnetism was strong. Guess why great monuments such as the Giza Pyramids, Stonehenge, and other sacred sites, which collected the natural electromagnetism of the Earth, were the centers of great civilizations where people could live in peace, health, and prosperity. Such is the beauty of knowing the benign and interconnected design of the universe.

The Dialogue

Joyce: Dear Reader, I wish that you could see what I am imagining in my mind. I see all beings, including the Earth, surrounded by bands of light filled with orbs sent from the sun, which dance around the Earth and all beings alive on the Earth in a symphony of mutual joy. It looks like a Disney movie of dandelion puffballs floating in rhythm to symphonic music. Indeed, it would be hard to be unhappy if one could just be at peace in these magnetic fields gently blowing across our lives.

But, speaking of what blew into my life, since you Peaceful One, are communicating with me now exist in the Blue Dimension, what is the Blue Dimension like?

Peaceful One: If one wanted to visit, it is not far away for it lines your skin from head to toe, expanding and contracting, as you need it. In short, you are living within it. You just can't perceive it without some specific intentions. We wrap the Blue Dimension like a blanket around every being so we can be as close to you as possible, and it takes all of us in all of the dimensions working together to create a manifestation in physical reality such as yourself. Think of us as a second skin and a peaceful one at that. Think of how communal we all are when you see the many layers of an onion or the segments of an orange.

Each layer of the cosmos and the human aura has its own inhabitants and code for referencing it. Those within the Blue layer are peaceful ones and serve as the souls of those who live on the physical dimension. The Blue Dimension is perfectly designed to be the layer between Earth and the more godlike realms. The intention for peace is the perfect access key for both remembering one's purpose to return to the higher dimensions, and to begin to access the next most available one, the Blue.

Within each layer, there is a point for both entry and exit. The Blue portal is above the head's energy vortex called the crown chakra. Those who use it often create for themselves a true beginning of a life lived on both dimensions. If one chooses to consciously function on just one layer or dimension, the energy transfers to the next in sleep. It is so common and easy a process that some come and go nightly through thought transference that shows up in dreams.

Edgar Cayce used the state between waking and sleeping as the Higher Mind entry point of his choice. There are many others, and each person has a blueprint as to which mode is of the best choice for them. Once a person has made the initial entry, there is the need to become a frequent flyer. Before one such entry is closed for lack of interest, there are those who need to be travelers of choice, not chance. The true interest of this author is not to be the reader of the whole record, but rather to be the leader of the charge to say: "Here is the hole in the wall; I've been in and out many times and it leads to great treasure, so come with me and I will show the way." After that you can go anywhere, anytime."

Joyce: Very good! So what I experience in a channeled reading is not just an imaginary thing, but is actually entering and leaving another dimension. And I do this within my aura, which has a Blue layer. And I need to keep the opening wide and free flowing by using it often and properly. Is that right?

Peaceful One: Yes, that is right! Whoopee! I think she's got it!

Joyce: OK, OK, let's not get too excited. I've been doing this for five years now and it's always been fun, but now, it's getting really interesting.

So let's get back to the issue of light. I know that when light is bent by passing through a crystalline structure, like a drop of water, a piece of glass, or a crystal, it splits into the colors of the rainbow. You seem to indicate that these colors are frequencies that have a lot of variations, which are matched to the needs of specific life forms. Are you saying that we all need all manner of rays of light and move from one ray to the next until we are so nurtured and full, that we enter the Presence of God?

Peaceful One: That is so, but do not ask me to describe the manner of light that you will find in the Presence of God, for it is of an ethereal kind and not for the making of rainbows as on Earth. Its frequency and vibration are very low, strong, and long lasting. Much is implanted in the planetary systems and channeled through the top of the Great Pyramid in Giza. For the pyramid's sides are sloped so as to collect Earth energy and to amass it so as to flow out of the top and curl and roll around it, engulfing the area and even the Earth itself. Above it was formed a giant intentional orb of peace, which radiated so much energy that it gave cause for joyful lifetimes. The pyramid is essentially a self-fulfilling mechanism of peace. It was constructed there for the precise purpose of promoting peace and calling forth from the next dimension the necessary means for peace to be accumulated and used for good, both in ancient times and today.

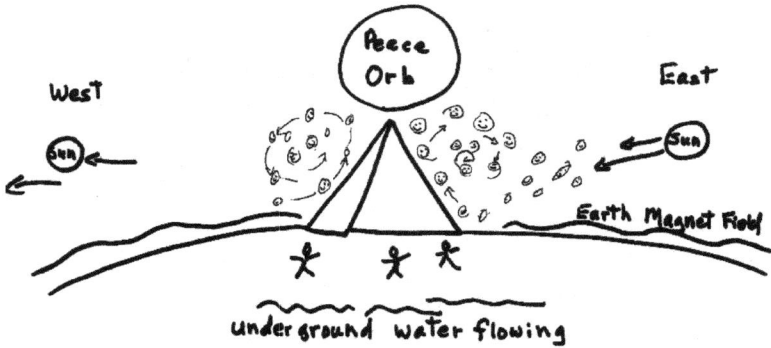

Drawing 5: Pyramid Collecting Earth's Magnetic Field

Joyce: So you are saying that the ancient Egyptians knew all about the portal to the next dimension and used it well?

Peaceful One: Would you like to write a book just on that topic and see what the wall murals are telling about the cultured ones who first sought to know what you are beginning to know now?

Joyce: Are my eyes blue? Does the sun rise each morning? Yes, yes and more yes. I would be so pleased to do so.

Peaceful One: OK, then it is an agreement and one that we made long ago, when you decided to go through the entry point to the earth dimension and return in faith to do this task. "I will resist nothing of Highest Good and will tell all that I see and hear." Thus is the reader's vow.

Joyce: I know that to accomplish such a feat, that I will have to be further healed, rejuvenated, pampered, prospered, loved and gifted so that my vibrations match the incoming vibrations. Oh darn, it's a tough job, but somebody has to do it. I wonder why more don't line up to volunteer. OK, I know that answer. They'd have to give up their fears and the limiting beliefs of the general society that fearful things actually exist outside their own minds. These days, I wouldn't hesitate for a minute, and besides, I have a feeling that I've done it before.

Chapter Four: The Human Aura

Dear Reader, as you have seen, the ancient Egyptians were well versed in their understanding of how the world worked. In fact, their whole society was founded upon the one simple principle called The Highest Good. To understand that, we would have to talk to a pharaoh who lived in the early times when it was most clearly used and their society was still in its development stages. I know that this seems insane to anyone who has not been reading this series from the beginning, but I am going to talk to the pharaoh called The Great Giver and ask him to explain how his role of pharaoh reflected the founding principle of the Highest Good. This is not his name used at that time as the language is now unknown. Later we find pharaohs named Tut Moses, I or II or II and later dynasties that are recorded, but this one is from many thousands of years before. He has arranged to communicate with us under the name Great Giver of the Highest Good or Great Giver for short. He says that his role was like a Justice of the Peace, making sure that society was given the Highest Good and nothing less. Before we start, however, remove all ideas from your mind about the rulers of early Egypt being cruel egomaniacs employing slaves for their selfish needs, for that is not the case. Shall we let him speak for himself?

The Perspective of Pharaoh: Great Giver

There is no need to identify me by my name or title or even a number, for I was, and am, no ruler as modern society thinks of a ruler. Please address me as the Great Giver of the Highest Good, or Great Giver for short.

In these very early days, there was no such thing as a succession of kings by lineage of birth as is currently thought. Each pharaoh came from the common people by invitation and choice. Therefore, there was no jealousy of who was born of whom and there was no thought of protecting a harem to assure biological parentage. For all were equal in all eyes, and none would supersede another for any reason. Indeed, I was born a simple farmer's son. I issued forth from my mother's womb as a tiny newborn in need of great care and suckling, as I was a weak baby. In our society, those who were the weakest were granted the greatest resources so that all would be strong contributors. Thus my mother was given the best of food and care so as to nurse me to full growth and stamina. This experience of the workings of the Highest Good principle was my first entrance into Egyptian society.

With this to be accomplished, there was the need for all to be educated in the principles of this peaceful society and the development of the understanding of the Higher Mind. For this, there were temple schools in which the children were educated in the right (Higher) mind and the lasting effects that it could create, leaving the topics of the lower mind to be reviewed for compliance with the Higher Mind. The entire process of entering the physical world, passing through the releases of grief, and the trusting of the Highest Good in all situations were depicted in story lines for the children to learn. Thus the tomb and temple walls were for this instruction and the long reign of the Higher Mind was depicted in great variety, size, and color. Symbols were used to tell stories about characters and were dramatized as would both entertain and instruct children, much like today's cartoon characters painted as heroes with superhuman powers.

With that accomplished, there was the need to learn a trade or skill. Each kindergarten child was selected for their unique traits and abilities to study something that would yield rich rewards for both them and society. Some were traders, as many foreigners came to discover the riches developed by the Egyptian use of the Highest Good. Foreigners marveled that Egypt, bereft of almost all resources except sand, sun, the Nile, river silt, and its people, created so much good. Other children were raised to be stonemasons, makers and keepers of documents, artists, teachers, farmers, wig makers, weavers, artists, bakers of bread, and brewers of beer, sailors, fishers, and all manner of skills and trades. None were asked to do undue labor more than another. Our goal was to serve the needs of all, and so all made a due contribution and all were served as was their need.

Lastly there was the need for a general administrator of the kind who truly understood the principle of the Highest Good and had experienced it in his or her own life. Therefore, they came to me as a small child and asked my Higher Mind to agree to the task of ruling in favor of the Highest Good for all, at all times and places, and nothing else. And indeed I said yes, for I had been created for just such a task. Therefore, I was taken to the scribes for a thorough education in the ancient texts, history, trade routes, foreign diplomacy, and the very complex set of rules and traditions regarding the distribution of resources such as food and water as well as labor. As a young man of twenty, with all of this having been learned over many years and with the full support of the many documentarians and administrators who promised to

76

support me and insure that I would not fail by my own means, we set forth with an acceptance ceremony, which is not to be confused with a coronation.

Actually, the tall round beehive hats were not crowns, but depictions of the grain bins which held the richest supply of stored grain that the world had ever seen, as such was needed to survive long seasons of drought, the longest being over twenty years. And so, as one walked about with such a headpiece, one was known as the giver of the grain and thus was supplied with all of the information needed to do a good job of supplying the weakest with the best and handling the many options for relief of need that were presented. Thus the story of the Wisdom of Solomon is a better representation of my daily duties than that depicted in modern movies.

Just as the distribution of goods was a duty, so was the direction of the work of the nation. Thousands of laborers depended on me to organize and plan the many feats of society such as building projects that were selected as doing the Highest Good for all. First the farm fields were constructed so as to absorb the flooding waters, retain them, and survive the dry season so as to most efficiently produce grain to feed the nation. In addition, the habits of the fish and the fowl were studied meticulously so as to cause huge schools and flocks to prosper, allowing us to take as many as we needed, but not so many as to diminish their reproduction. In addition, the weathering of many of the rocks were observed to determine the nature of each type of rock including the erosion capacity of some to provide minerals and diatomaceous earth for its many benefits and others to stand for time undisturbed by weather or erosion. Thus, even the rock itself was a resource to be utilized for the good and to minimize unnecessary labor.

Finally, there was the need to form funerary processions, for the death of one was the prospect of a returning life in the future. Those who passed out of this existence were treasured for their experience and skill and were heartily invited to return in good stead as a new child in our society. Thus many did arrive with memories of prior lifetimes intact, bringing the rich resources of skills and abilities. Such agreements between the living and recently departed gave us great continuity of learning and skills.

As this has been a shortened version of much more that will be given later, it would seen ideal to end with the statement that in our society, it was a requirement that each have a healthy and happy life, as that was required of all to maintain a healthy society. Thus the human aura was indeed well known to us and we wore the colored collars as an exhibit of how it surrounded not only our heads, but also our whole body. In being able to access our Higher Minds, we were advanced in the art of mental viewing and daily accessed this ability to fully see what was going on in each other's auras. With this skill, we could advise each other as to the correction of an intention or attitude that might later turn into a demise of some kind, which would affect us all. In fact, it was the duty of the mother, wife, or woman of a household or office to see her own aura and correct it as well as those of her associates. Women were found to be better than men at creating benign fields of energy that impacted others.

With this we will pause and let the entire list of characteristics of two types of people be outlined in this chapter so that the reader, who is so dear to me as well, can see how many different traits are reflected in each person's aura.

+*+

Joyce: Wow is not a very big word for such a description, but what else can one say? From this description of the job of pharaoh, I can see how the good of all was the guiding intention and meant that the least capable was the best served as Christ was quoted as saying in the Gospel: "The first shall be last and the last first." And clearly the health of the individual was closely watched and guarded. Apparently, they thought that the health of the body was determined by the attitudes and intentions as seen in the aura and they could see the aura with the Third Eye, which is a term used by Hindu traditions to refer to mental viewing of non physical realities. It is what Medical Intuitionists use to see inside the human body. If the aura showed only good and assuming good nutrition, then the body would be healthy.

Well, then, let's take a better look at the Human Aura and see what we can learn to understand what they knew and used. For this section, I will summarize what the Hathors have given to me in various short readings.

The Hathor's Description of the Human Aura

The human aura or body of light is the higher vibrational part of our body. It consists of layers of differing energy, usually depicted as layers of color. It is the non-physical womb of the body's existence in which it lives. It is complete with an energetic amniotic fluid, which can be seen as gently flowing light. It has spinning energy umbilical cords called chakras, which feed and protect the body through constant exchanges of energy. The body never leaves it. If the aura and its spinning vortexes function well, the body is healthy. If the aura is not healthy, the body experiences illness and eventually has to miscarry the physical parts of the body, even though the aura continues on, fully capable of producing yet another body.

The aura contains all of the information and energy necessary for souls to live in both spirit and human experience. It is the local seat of each soul. A person is surrounded with it at all times and, since one never leaves it, each is nourished by it, healed by it, reformed and rejuvenated by it. People are protected by it and can continue on forever with its constant recycling of the giving and receiving of energy from and to the Blue Dimension. It consists of assimilation and elimination of energy. The body assimilates Blue energy from the Blue Dimension and eliminates or donates energy it does not need anymore. Without the constant incoming and outgoing energy, the human body does and will shrivel and die.

For this part of the study, refer to the front cover of the book and look carefully at the colorful layers around the physical body of a human actively engaged in physical life. The aura depicted shows a person with an active Conscious Mind. Later I will describe one quite different, that of a quiet and peaceful one, whose Conscious Mind is very cooperative with the Higher Mind.

The outer shell of the aura, which is usually about a meter away from the skin, is like a turtle eggshell, flexible and tough. Its function is to open the soul's presence to life on the physical plane. It has pores for the coming and going of energy and it converts the incoming Blue energy to the Green energy needed to function in the Earth dimension. When the soul wishes to withdraw from the earthly body, the shell reverses the energy, turning Green back to Blue and the soul continues on with all of the memories and skills it acquired in physical experience. Since the presence of God is everywhere, there is plenty of life energy for this dual existence so that a soul can create a human lifetime in a human body, complete with a Conscious Mind while remaining active in the Blue Dimension. Essentially, the purpose of a human lifetime is to bring a unique expression of the Divine into time and space and then to reunite the physical dimension with the Blue. To make a comparison, we are volunteer pioneers to claim this dimension as a time and place for our particular expression of the Presence of God.

+

Joyce: I have to stop here and explore a question. If we, as humans, experience a diminished form of the Presence of God with our Conscious Minds in the little world of our aura, how do we interact with other humans having similar experiences, for example, in the building of relationships, families, societal structures, and the like?

Peaceful One: How does anyone engage in any experience except through a wholly internal process, much like seeing the moonlight on the water come to your feet on one beach, while another sees it coming to their feet on another beach?

Joyce: What? Do you mean to say that just like seeing the moon on the beach, that painful experiences of fear and misery are also completely individual for each person? It is only experienced within one's own aura?

Peaceful One: Yes! Consider that the sun and moon keep shining whether there is war or peace upon the Earth. Fear and harm is a completely localized, internal experience for humans. Even if one intends harm to you and actually does harm to you, you still have the choice to see it as good and avoid the belief that you are unloved and deserving of harm. If you avoid that belief, then you cannot be harmed. You will only be given good, even if the good is to see all good restored to you after it has been taken away. Remember the story of Job.

Joyce: OK, now let me see, does that mean that no matter what happens, that I can chose to see it as good and thus be open to the Presence of God? Every time you explain this to me, it is truly mind bending. Everything seems opposite. It would take a Jedi to get this right. What good is such a world? Why do we want to even take the chance of experiencing pain at all?

Peaceful One: Why not? If you can create the good, why not create the pain as well? At least that is the thought of the ancient ones mentioned in the Bible as fallen angels who were given creative free will and decided to unleash evil into their own lives and others who agreed to do the same. At last we now have peace making some progress in the gradual disclosure of the true nature of this experience called pain. For it is the choice of the experiencer and their nature of creating either pain or peace for themselves. And in doing so, they contribute to the soup of human experience which either supports the pain or eliminates it through lack of interest. It is like children who decide to crayon on the walls and, when they see the distress that it causes, decide never to do it again. Could a Jedi be so trained as to turn all harm away just by refusing to be fearful? What fun would that be?

Joyce: So did I choose to create pain for myself when I decided to enter into a human experience?

Peaceful One: No, no one decides to create pain, rather they accepted some of it for the sake of resisting fear in sufficient quantities that they would be able to open to a better understanding that would turn the tide of human existence and make the soup of human experience so good that the fallen angels might return to peace after all. They had to come to Earth to be part of this, for it is one of the last places where pain can exist. They all have a great amount of support from all of the other peaceful places and beings offering great gifts, support, and assistance.

Joyce: I'm going to have to think about this, but I can see how important it is to see the relationship between the soul and the human experience and the truth of the existence of the communication between them. Let's go on, please.

+

Hathors: The outer layer of the human aura is roughly egg shaped, but still can have many variations of that shape. For example, people more active in the Conscious Mind are bulgy at the top and more peaceful people are narrow at the top. The outer layer must always be intact for the body and mind to function properly, but it is also permeable and interacts with the energy around it. People who have severe mental illnesses have disruptions in this outer layer and cannot use their minds properly. The layer, however, can be repaired and great improvement seen with a little meditation from family and friends sitting in a circle around the individual. The healing circle participants connect with their own blue layers and ask for the healing be given to the injured one who can merely lay asleep in the middle. It is a most loving act to perform.

In addition, those who have bulgy tops can reform them by being in the same circle and asking for peace from the unusual energy flows. These meditation circles were once very common upon the Earth. The most recent example is the practices of the American Indians who danced around the campfire reciting the old songs of peace. Many were healed, even if they did not have full knowledge of how and why they were doing the dances. We only wish that the remaining tribes would realize that they could cure the genetic tendency to alcoholism with the same technique, if they apply the specific intention to do so.

Although this outer layer is usually not of much trouble, it is always opening and closing its pores for the inhalation and exhalation of the cosmic energy of peace. Thus its pliability and permeability is of importance. Should one never experience the peace of a summer evening or the gentle rain on the roof, one might not take in enough of the energy of nature, nor expel enough grief. Thus we remind all, that the presence of the natural environment is a primary source of healing for everyone and it should not be underestimated.

There is a constant flow of grace through this shell, and thus the body, as long as it is pliable (adequate water, flexible thinking, open heart, tissues massaged, bones adjusted). Like electricity, this energy flows where there are good connections and a conductive environment (a mildly alkaline PH is for the body the ideal electrolyte balance of bodily fluids). The bones and nerves are points of contact that need to be aligned for a smooth flow of energy. If a junction between bones is disrupted, the energy cannot flow to the next junction and so a part of the body is starved by that disruption. The more you ask for this life energy, the more you are open to it so more is given because you become more permeable or open. The function of castor oil is to condition the aura energy, thus allowing energy to rebalance and make good connections within the layers of the aura.

There is a tube of golden light that conveys energy orbs from the sun throughout the body. The Pranic Tube opens the top of the aura and conveys energy orbs around inside the outer shell, circling around it and feeding it life energy. The energy then travels through all of the layers and forms a cone above the head of the physical body, sending orbs of life energy to and from the crown chakra through the spinal nervous system to the feet and around the bottom of the aura where it circulates around the aura again.

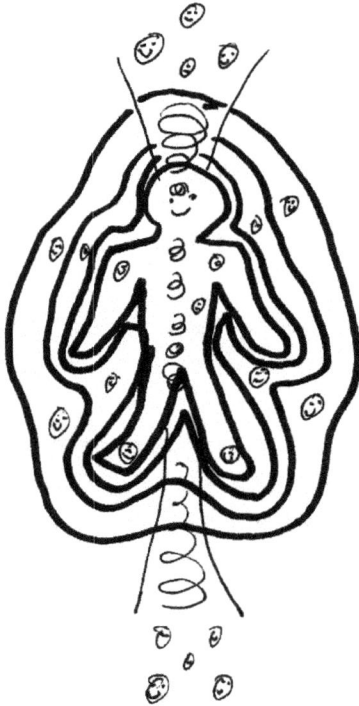

Drawing 6: The Human Aura Shell and Pranic Tube

The pranic tube is the major conveyor of God's presence and its gift of life. To have it closed is disastrous and to have it unfolding open is a form of evolution to higher life. The energy of the pranic tube flows through the spinal cord to the feet and rolls and circles outward forming cascades of energy, which surround the body. This cascading energy can be improved with the addition of castor oil on the palms of the hands and the heels of the feet so as to better electrify each organ of the body with the circulating grace of God. Cayce suggested a device that connects wires to the hands and feet called the Radiac Device that does the same thing. The pranic tube is the direct conduit from God through the solar system's aura, to the Earth's aura, through that to each person's aura. The pranic tube passes through all layers of the aura, giving each is own special vibrations.

The next layer just inside of the outer shell is white with mixtures of colors including yellow. This layer stores patterns from past lives as well as experiences, tendencies, and latent abilities. These past life patterns are all available to you for the asking. These past life resources are not like old history books or DVD games to replay what was done in the past, but rather are for the use of the soul to reestablish itself in a new growth pattern in a new lifetime. For instance, there might be the ability to play music or to use math effectively or even to be a leader. Once an individual accesses these memories, they will be made available in ever increasing quantity and quality. It may sound incredible for modern society to consider but for the ancients, these stored memories were a rich resource from which to draw for the benefit of great societies. Thus there were many methods used to explore this layer. The few modern explorers, who have the courage to face who and what they have been in the past and to use these experiences in a productive manner, will discover that humans are far more capable than they thought.

A good method of accessing these memories is to imagine the color yellow with a movie running backward on the screen of life. Once one reaches the end of the recollections of the Conscious Mind, then turn the movie machine to automatic and take a nap. Upon awakening, one will find that one's abilities are amazingly easy to access with just a thought or conscious request. Once one has learned to access these memories, it does not take a hypnotist to tell one that they have been alive before.

The next layer inward from the white layer is the Interactive Layer. This multicolored layer is depicted as many tiny layers all acting as one. Being as this is the major layer of connection with the universe in terms of this lifetime, it is a busy intersection of conversation: Help and assistance come and go in an exchange of energy between the soul and the current lifetime and its body. It is the ideal area to show the incoming joy and the outgoing grief relief as the healing process goes forward. It is the place of bliss experiences for the human body as it is relieved of pain and suffering and given the more pure and fine energy of the soul.

The soul resides in the next dimension, called the Blue Dimension, and creates the current lifetime in the body. It is the point of cooperation between the Soul and the Conscious Mind for the purpose of giving the soul's unique expression of the Divine to a new time and experience, thus the bliss. Being of the Blue Dimension, this is a band of blue light.

When one determines to open to communication with their soul in a conscious way, this layer becomes very active, as thoughts and intentions zip back and forth between the soul and human conscious mind in conversation. The more that the layer is used in this way, the more efficient it becomes until there is a blending of the two minds and thus the conscious mind becomes fully developed by the soul. Through this interaction, the conscious mind can cooperate and fully participate in the life plan using the vast resources of the Higher Mind of the soul. There are various methods for achieving this access, but once one realizes that it has been going on all of their life in a subliminal way, they can focus on it and make it entirely conscious.

Along with the information transfer, there is a spectrum of other energies that are transferred back and forth, which constitute the removal of fear and illness and the application of rejuvenating energy. Therefore, one who actively channels their soul is also effecting their own healing and rejuvenation. This occurs more or less automatically, unless they retain their fears and limiting beliefs.

This dark blue layer also contains the negative blueprint of the soul's path and is the place of the giving of life energy to the inner layers. Some people spontaneously see bright blue circles in their visual field called blue pearls. Blue pearl contact with the soul is described here as little blue spirals of light from the blue dimension that are opening and closing and infusing life energy. These events are openings to this blue level of the aura as seen by the eye. This blue level, of course, connects with the pranic tube, which runs through the aura and body connecting Heaven and Earth. This is where the intention for the Highest Good organizes all functions. Thus all channelers or dimensional tubing practitioners, as Joyce calls them, are reformed, healed, prospered, and directed to the Presence of God because they opened to their blue layer and its connection to the pranic tube. This opening can be upgraded, refined, and constantly evolved as one desires to be happy and happier yet. Since the original benign blueprint of perfection is always there, the body can be restored to this design by intentional use of this energy. The energy field will even function if a body part has been amputated. The energy field of an amputated limb is still operating and providing the experience of the missing limb. If properly intentioned, this energy field can regrow the amputated tissues. Those who come and inquire will be given directions.

The pink or rose layer is inside the blue layer and is where relationships within and without take place. Relationships which are balanced in giving and receiving, and thus healthy, glow a warm pink, those that are unbalanced and disastrous turn a warm rose with some yellow. This layer of relationships includes a colorful display of your relationship with all others, the earth, nature, and all experiences that you have. These relationships should be peaceful for health to be maintained. It is in this layer that love of all types is experienced. If the Conscious Mind participates in the lifestyle of the Highest Good, this layer remains healthy and love brings joyous energy. This joy prompts one to use one's abilities in the service of others, which brings even more joy.

The yellow multicolored layer is inside of the pink layer and is where thoughts and words affect the physical body. It is the seat of the individual personality. Doubts and negative thinking in this layer can cause restrictions in life

90

energy by closing the pores of this layer to the infusion of life from the blue layer and disrupting relationships in the pink layer. If they are closed, the life giving vibrations of the blue layer and the pranic tube cannot penetrate freely. This is an area of great interest to health care workers because, what the patient is thinking and feeling about themselves and their condition, can block much good that could otherwise be accessed within their own aura.

For example, if a person is ill, a health care worker should be sensitive to how he or she thinks about him or herself. What name does a client or patient call him or herself? How are their relationships? How do they treat themselves? The content of these thoughts and labels creates conditions in the body to conform to these thoughts. These conditions can be very specific. For example if a patient calls himself the indecisive one, then his legs will not have confidence as to where to go and they will have illness or disability. If a patient calls herself a wondrous self-healing organism of peace, then the many organs and systems of the body vibrate at the level where this can occur. Simply by treating patients with respectful, loving concern and speaking to them in encouraging words, a health care worker can clear out this layer of much doubt and negativity and thus allow much self healing to occur that consists entirely of natural flows of life energy in the patient's own aura field.

This multicolored layer is also where emotions are kept active through repetitive thinking, causing further influence on the body, either pain and poor functioning of organs or joyful acceptance of one's gift of existence and release of fear. This is where the essential function and importance of forgiveness is illustrated. For it is when we let go of the need to constantly feed ourselves negative thoughts (which cause negative emotions) that this area changes to joy and happiness. If we do not forgive, then there is a barrier to the life giving energies of the blue layer and pranic tube. These positive or negative emotions cause the chakras to open or close. Therefore the body will only receive what this layer will allow through its pores (chakras). And so if no new life giving energy comes through, then the body feeds off its own energy, replicating damaged cells, until it dies. Indeed, each organ has its own chakra. Each emotion affects a particular organ through the opening or closing of the chakra of that organ. Therefore releasing the specific negative thought pattern blocking the flow of life energy to that particular organ or body part can heal specific illness.

These two layers, the yellow and multicolored layer are where the Conscious Mind functions. As your Conscious Mind releases fear and installs joy, these unblocked layers provide a compatible interface with the pranic tube and the blue layer, thus your life prospers according to the Highest Good which is organizing, feeding and operating the whole energy system.

Another small electric blue layer is next to the skin. This is the closest interface between the skin and the soul and where the Conscious Mind is brought into complete, peaceful cooperation. If the yellow multicolored layer allows, it joins with the outer, larger blue layer for complete health that is virtually indestructible.

There are vessels and tubules between this thin electric blue layer next to the skin and the pores of the skin, allowing assimilation and elimination of energy. Massage and oils can help the skin and all of its sensitive layers to function well as conductors of incoming and outgoing energy. Again, castor oil so conditions the energy and skin that it allows spirals of both assimilation and elimination to rebalance and thus heal the body. An interesting sensation is caused when the active opening and closing of skin cells in the thin blue layer causes a tingling, tickling, or crawling feeling on the skin. Another sensation of aura energy, is the pleasurable sensation that a sunbath gives through direct exposure to sunlight which charges this layer with additional energy as the orbs from the sun directly feeds the body with life in all of its multicolored facets of light. A sunbath need not be long. Brief, but daily exposure is entirely sufficient.

All of these layers are connected, organized and, controlled through the top of the pranic tube. If it is open and accepting, all goes well. If one doubts God's love for oneself, it narrows and starves the whole system. Thus treating a patient with loving patience and kindness such as God gives, encourages the pranic tube to open wider and thus many can be healed just with the reminder that they are loved by God. Giving saline solution, Epsom salt baths, or an oil rub can cure some discomforts by opening pores and hydrating the tissues with alkaline balancing substances. In all cases, fear and disrespect, if accepted by the patient, closes down the system, starving it of life giving energy.

Drinking sufficient water allows energy to better flow within the body and through the layers. If too little water is present, the energy is sticky and non conductive. If relaxed, tendons, ligaments, and muscles allow energy to flow through normal channels, if they are not relaxed, there are spasms and areas of bunched up energy, resulting in starvations of successive organs, which depend on these channels for their flow of life energy and repair instructions. Yoga, massage, and chiropractic are useful openers of energy channels. Bones, In particular, have points of connection that need to be aligned. A joint that does not make a good connection between bones or has a bunching of energy in the ligaments or nerves can starve the tissues from that point outward to the periphery of the body as outlined by the nervous system. A blockage of the flow of life energy at any point can starve organs and major systems, thus creating diseases of insufficiency. Blockages of elimination of used energy can cause an overabundance of energy and toxins causing illnesses of over supply or toxicity.

Acupuncture needles are highly conductive and can stimulate a skin chakra to open and connect the body chakras with the blue layers. Peaceful energy such as Reiki floods the aura with Higher Mind energy. Energy workers with peace on their minds can touch an area and cause it to open or to relax or even can push energy around for rebalancing. Medical Intuitive procedures ask the Conscious Mind to release a specific negative belief and strongly ask the soul to take over the healing function with more strength, using the permission of the Conscious Mind of the patient.

Music is a universal healing method. Movement of the body in dance, singing or playing of musical instruments as well as physical therapy opens up channels of energy flows. Music permeates the whole system and opens and rebalances gently. Each person has his or her own healing melody, based on his or her prior lifetimes and plan for this lifetime. Each organ and chakra has its own naturally healthy note. An intuitive musician receiving direction from his or her own Higher Mind can literally sing or musically play a body back to health as the chakras and organs vibrate to wholesome sounds. The use of healing music was common in ancient Egypt and can be revived when those interested apply their talents and intentions. The Great Oneness delights greatly in giving such healing modalities.

Colored lights, ultrasound, weak electric currents, magnetism, and infrared and ultraviolet light can affect healing on the energetic level of the aura. Doing creative and peaceful activities and thinking peaceful thoughts can also influence healing. Listening to the sounds, smells, and feelings of nature can bring in Higher Mind energy and open the pranic tube. Herbs, scents and stones are helpful influences for the relief of grief and the absorption of joy. Clearly an open and peaceful mind is of great health value.

Foods and the fasting from foods have the effect of supporting more absorption or elimination. Thus the below-ground foods such as potatoes cause elimination of fears and stabilize the belief in good. The above-ground foods such as lettuce cause more change and openings to occur. Some illnesses require more or less of one type of food or the other. If one does a daily guidance reading for one's health, they will be given instructions for their perfect nourishment. This guidance, which comes from the large blue layer, will align with their unique needs so well, that vast qualities of relief from grief and fear are experienced in small comfortable steps. These readings, as were done daily in ancient times, yield the infusion of much grace, joy, and happiness. If good conditions can be consistently maintained, all bodily functions will perfectly balance, causing the body to heal and rejuvenate. Death will occur not because of disease or aging, but by the choice of the Soul to bring the body into cooperation with the desire for a new experience. A new experience will require a new body, thus the old one will be sloughed off and a new one formed.

The master healer of all is meditation, which is a concentrated intention to be at peace and to connect with one's own Higher Mind. Meditation is the profound relaxation of the Conscious Mind and implies the willingness to hear guidance and to follow it. When one meditates – or even sleeps – one relaxes the muscles allowing the bones to connect, the nerves to fire, and organs to function. In meditation, one enters into contact with the blue layer, where Higher Mind has openings for life giving energy. In addition, third eye seeing takes place in meditation with its many benefits of transmission of helpful knowledge. In meditation, there is a feeling of bliss, which vibrates life energy through the whole system, sometimes turning the whole aura blue.

The universal cause of all illness is fear in all of its many forms; fear of living, dying, being in relationship, not being in relationship, injury, lack of ability, future events, etc. It includes doubt of all things Higher Mind, judgment of self or others, rigid expectations, anger, stubbornness, resistance to good, skepticism, depression, grief, regret, greed, conflict, envy, and intention to do harm to oneself or others. Fear constricts energy flows and closes up chakras either starving the body of life energy or refusing to give up the elimination of toxins.

Each of us brings patterns of fear from past lives as well as acquires more through life experiences, so the release of fears is an essential task. Thus the process of healing often involves reviewing these experiences over and over so as to assure oneself, that one has always been safe and sound within one's own aura soul shell and that all of one's experiences, both positive and negative, lead unerringly to the Presence of God. This type of review and release of grief can be obtained by a daily health reading with one's Peaceful One such as was suggested for the selection of food. The habit of patiently observing and accepting the difficulties of life as a potentially positive experience is optimum.

We are all designed to bring the Presence of God into physical existence within our own life, body and relationships. We are all connected through the vibrational pool of life. The intention for the Highest Good is the only viable way to live, for it opens us to our Higher Mind and protects us from all harm. It is with this sense of security and optimum health that we can release all fear and become the beings of light that we are.

+*+

Joyce: I think you just talked me into never having any fears again. If I do allow fears, I starve myself of essential energy and start to deteriorate from the inside out. That sounds like a definition of cancer and the immune system diseases that are rampant today. I so wish that everybody could understand this and never have to suffer disease of any kind. But that would require a great level of peacefulness. What would an aura that was peaceful look like?

97

Hathors: For us to describe it, we'd have to call it a perfect blue marble with swirls of peacefully moving weather. It is an interesting comparison to the view of earth from space that is so loved, is it not?

When a person is fully engulfed in the energy of the Blue Dimension or the white iridescent layer of the Contented Ones, they swirl around in unison as the moments of experience come and go, and the body, the soul and all other co-inhabitants of the life experience expand their consciousness to be both receivers and givers of light. This is pretty much what we look like. Thus we have named this book Being of Light to provide an ample description of who you/we are as well. Welcome to our world as we are all, indeed, one.

Joyce: Oh! I can just imagine my aura as a blue marble flowing in peace just like the Earth rotates peacefully in space. Well, turn on the blue light special for me. You've convinced me to never allow fear and to always remain peaceful. As Dr. Seuss once said: "Oh, what a great adventure we will have."

Chapter Five: Heal Your Aura, Heal Your Body

Peaceful One: How about a good long rest? You have just returned from two days of work on the road and aren't you just exhausted?

Joyce: No actually, I'm not exhausted. I admit that I went to bed really early last night, but I am up and happily energized to go to a family funeral. My aunt on my mother's side passed away at 89. She was very frail and did not recover from an infection.

Peaceful One: Doesn't that make you wonder about energy in the human body? How is it made to be available to the body and why do some have lots of it and some very little? How does one grow old and frail and another live in health for over one hundred years?

Joyce: Well, that is a good topic indeed, considering the weekend that I just had. We had Ellen and Denise come to the farm for a presentation of Energy Medicine. It is a system of understanding the energy flows of the human body that was developed by Donna Eden. Ellen and Denise were so impressed with the value of this system, that they studied it deeply and give classes and sessions that have astounding results. I had Denise do a treatment on me because I had been feeling tired and tense. She did a clearing of my field of energy, which she called the asteroid belt. She said that people who do a lot of forgiveness and releases of pain and suffering need to clear this area of the debris of these experiences. I have to guess that it was the yellow, multicolored layer you described earlier.

She set her intention to clear the area and then used her hand in the air in figure eights to whisk the area. I could actually feel my body change as she did so. My back and right side twinged and then relaxed. My legs cramped and then relaxed. I could feel a better blood flow and a shiver of energy flow through me. Afterwards, I rested and then took a walk. My bones seemed to fit into place better. Energy flowed easily and I did not get tired from the exercise. The change was mostly around my waist and I felt less congested there. At any rate, it was thrilling to know that I could lighten the load on my body of all of the old pain and move freely and happily once again.

Would you comment on that experience?

Peaceful One: Would you comment on my being in my body at peace with the fact that all experiences are a coming and going thing and that some experiences that are hateful at first can be transformed into love and set free?

Joyce: You in your body? What do you mean? You are in spirit form. You don't have a body, do you?

Peaceful One: Of which body do you speak? Do you mean the physical body of bone and muscle or the energy body, which surrounds your physical body and energizes it, giving life each moment? Indeed I am in that energy body, same as you.

Joyce: You are talking about the human aura, I assume. Some people can see it and it even can be measured on instruments. Humans have an energy field around them that is evident to some of our senses, but not all. I remember in one class that I did, that I took two metal wires and bent them into a right angle and lightly held one in each hand so that they would swing at will. I walked around and they would swing together and cross when I went close to a human body, crossing at the chakra points. I suppose these wires are called dousing rods, and they are so simple and easy to use, that people have been using them to find water, buried artifacts, and all sorts of things for millennia. Is this what you are talking about?

Peaceful One: Notice how simple and peaceful these rods are to use and how much useful information they can give. Would you not be amazed that they were left as a gift from the Highest Good?

Yes, my dearest one, your energy body is my place of residence when we are in incarnation. You can think of me as your neighbor in your "energyhood" so to speak.

Joyce: Wow, I thought that you were a long way away in Heaven or something. You mean that you are right beside me, going through all of these experiences right along with me? Do you carry some of the debris of the painful experiences and feel the need to get rid of them? Interesting!

Peaceful One: How could I have been a long way away and know you as well as I do?

Joyce: Well that changes everything. I can no longer think of myself as alone having a tough life experience. Nor can I think of you as being uncompassionate about what I am experiencing because you have to experience it as well.

Peaceful One: Well, then, let's not be two, but one forever more. Let's use our pronouns interchangeably and learn how to love and care for each other in peace. And please to not send me to any more depressing places such as being alone in a dark house when you come home from work. I want the lights on and a happy face greeting me at the door with a warm hug. And I want it for you as well. Do you want to do that for me or for you, or whoever we really are?

Joyce: Well, yes, of course. I have to think about this. Have I been subjecting you to depression? I knew that I was suffering from that and needed to work myself out of it, but I did not think that you would suffer as well. How are you doing with it?

Peaceful One: About as well as you are. Did you not think that wherever you go, I go, and whatever you experience, I experience, as it says in the Long Story? Did you think that you did not count? That I did not count? Did you think that you were alone or ever truly could be?

Joyce: Yes, I did think that. Well, this changes everything. OK, so let's go back to the beginning. When I first heard you in the sunny window, you were just inches from my skin. I'm not even going to ask if you've been there all of my life for I know that the answer is yes, but why is it that I wasn't more aware of you?

Peaceful One: Wasn't there another being there with us then? Remember the Fearful One? At that time you were spending a lot of time with that one and little with me. Over time, you quit inventing the Fearful One and listened only to me. And look where that has gotten you.

Joyce: Yes, indeed, but if I invented the Fearful One, did I also invent you as well?

Peaceful One: Did the Fearful One have the power to keep you alive from moment to moment? Did the Fearful One heal you of your health problems and lead you to better friends and work relationships? Do you think that the Fearful One had that power?

Joyce: No, most certainly not. The Fearful One always made me feel tired and depressed. It was like having an energy vampire taking my life out of me in little sips. You, on the other hand, gave me hope, healing, and a new life. I don't think that the Fearful One could have a life of its own without giving it my attention. But you brought me more energy whenever I needed. Yes, there is quite a difference between the two.

Peaceful One: Then how could the depressed feelings hang around our energy home for so long since neither one of us wanted them?

Joyce: Good question. How?

Peaceful One: Perhaps, we'd better give a better explanation of how the energy field that we live in works. Have you enjoyed participating in a much better type of reading material this time? Would you like to do some more diagrams and show your Dear Readers what we mean by energy fields and how to heal themselves?

Joyce: OK, I am up for this. I have felt it to be very important in my life and I like this feeling of being able to discard the energy vampire from my energy home. I see how you can bring me all of the energy that I need, so I, too, can live a long and healthy life. I agree, a long reading on healing the human aura is in order. Let's go for it!

Reading: Healing the Human Aura

Peace and Light Association
Peaceandlight01@aol.com
Peaceandlight.net
Copyright, 2013

Without further ado, there is one thing to understand about the human aura that was not made clear before. Once an intention is placed upon the magnetic waves of energy coming and going into and out of the aura, there is no need to do anything else. Once one has made a change in the aura layers with a positive intention to be happy, immediately there is an opening to the Higher Mind to do its job of healing and perfecting all of the layers in a strong structure for sustaining life. For one to understand this effect, compare it to an orange that is punctured, causing the inner juices to begin to flow outward. Once that energy flows, there is a long chain of events, which causes the demise of the fruit. The same holds true of the lifeblood lost from a damaged vein or artery. But if the integrity of the whole is maintained, both the orange and artery can continue life for a very long time.

Therefore, it is imperative that one does not injure one's aura field by trying too hard to be perfect or trying to repair oneself at the cost of some damage to be sustained in the process. Rather, the repair can be conducted at once with the intention that the true health that the being was originally created to have, be put back in place. That would be the intention for the Highest Good, meaning no harm and much, much good. It could be as simple as to repeat to oneself consciously the following: "I want to be whole, happy, healthy, and loved at all times." If this was said without doubt and in a happy state of mind, then nothing else is necessary, as the heavens are filled with all of the right stuff for much health and happiness. It only waits to be admitted.

In fact, that is the intact condition of infants when they are first born. If no fears that they will be harmed are introduced, they will continue on in peace and nothing will harm them at all. If this is hard to believe, just look at the long-lived oak trees, which have small seeds, but hard shells, which few predators can penetrate. Left alone to produce its own designed form of life, it will do so and the same is true of the human body. Thus this reading is essentially a test of the faith of the readers to admit to themselves that they have had fear in their hearts and that removing those fears will lead them to a complete return to health and long life.

So, let us proceed with confidence, for this reading to have been made at all, the true intention for the Highest Good had to be in place for a long time. Should another negative or doubtful intention come along, the readings would vanish completely or be so distorted that no one could read them or understand what was being said. Should one read the same intention over and over again in one's mind and heart each moment of each day and accept no other intention, then much would be accomplished that is good. It is not to be expected that it will occur instantaneously or never be proven wrong, but rather that it builds and builds, as fears are cleared out and more positive intentions are added each time.

In the interest of saving time, there is one clear and positive way to illustrate this principle. Should one have a fall and suffer a small scrape on one's elbow, one merely says to oneself: "Those scrapes heal themselves as I have seen over and over again in childhood." Therefore a person thinks nothing of it and all of the energy that is needed would be admitted to heal that scrape and the skin would be repaired and refreshed in perfect condition (except maybe being a little tougher to save the trouble of doing it again). Would this not make a beautiful model for all illness and disease? Just call up a local Medical Intuitive and ask them to assist your intention so that it is strong and clear and think nothing of it. So much good can be done this way.

You might be interested to know that not far from the skin of a potato is a similar aura and when the potato wishes to grow itself into a new plant, the aura sends out a signal, which forms into a growth of a new shoot intending to grow a whole new plant capable of bearing many more potatoes. It does so by having a need to reproduce and the life aura begins to supply growth energy to transmute the old form into a new one. Thus in making this connection, one might call oneself a growth potato instead of a couch potato. For even a vegetable of little movement is a place of transmission of life energy of the highest kind. In this case, the potato lives free of fear and grows as designed. Thus we leave the reader with yet another solution to a human problem. The reason for human pain and suffering is to be found only a short distance into the aura field, for the blockages of fear and doubt are to blame. One should be glad to be as free of fear as a couch or rather a growth potato, after all.

+

Joyce: I think that I get this. My friend, Jim, who is a wonderful Medical Intuitive, keeps several books that list the harmful beliefs associated with specific illnesses. When a client comes to him with a specific illness, he looks up the false belief and reads it to them. If they recognize it and agree to release it, they are halfway to their healing. If they then replace it with the thought of the Highest Good, then they have completed their own healing. The makings of perfect health are always within our own aura. We only need to clean out the fearful, unloving, harmful thoughts. It is sort of like washing mud off of your beautiful car. Jim thought of it as opening the Cosmic Health Channel. He loved it.

So let me think about how we are to do that. Does it make a difference if the fear is unrecognized?

Peaceful One: Yes and no. All that is needed is to know that it is fear and that it should have no place in your being... our Being of Light that is.

Joyce: If one makes the effort to give up one's grief and false beliefs, how long does it take to be healed?

Peaceful One: Why don't you tell me? How long have you had the belief that others will never support you? How has it injured your life, your heart and your body? And how have you managed to relieve it?

Joyce: Well, I've held it a long time, at least 50 years. It caused me to have subpar relationships one after the other. I am still releasing it to be sure but so far, I find that it happens in little steps. It's like peeling the layers of an onion and having the stinging juice evoke tears. After each peeling of a layer, there is a resting period in which the new thinking is incorporated and then the next layer is opened up. I guess it does eventually come to an end, but I haven't seen it yet. I suppose it fades away for lack of interest as you often say.

Peaceful One: How has what I have had to say helped you?

Joyce: You have been patient, kind, and helpful. You never criticize me or chastise me. In short, you love me.

Peaceful One: Well then, let's just continue exchanging love until you are fully healed, for it is different for each person and even each issue. In the meantime, I love loving you and you love being loved. Even when we don't have any issues to heal, we'll still be whole, happy, and healthy in every way. We don't ever have to stop. We'll be so strong that only the bad leaks out and all of the good is safe inside. How's that for a plan?

Joyce: OK by me. I'll love it, start to finish. I may have to take my car through the car wash over and over, but at least you go with me. Sigh, you did it again. You found my pain and replaced it with hope and joy. I love you, you know.

Peaceful One: Ditto.

Chapter Six: Just a Little Bit of Joy

Joyce: I am so encouraged that we can all heal ourselves by giving up grief that I wanted to know what it looks like in the aura when it happens. How would I know for sure that it had happened? Could I know it, feel it, see it? How would I feel?

Peaceful One: Since the aura is a system of layers of light, there are many weavings of thought and emotion and once one very high thought enters and begins to command all else, then everything changes from a dull greenish blue to the spectacular color of gold. When this occurs, there is the emotion of joy. So your sign that you are healing is joy.

Joyce: I have felt joy and been happy, but then I would move to another feeling. For me it is a long cycling in and out of joy and happiness followed by sadness. I think that I heal one issue and feel joy and then another issue comes up and I have to feel the pain of it, work through it, and then the joy comes again.

Peaceful One: Very well described, so let me explain that joy is not the same as being happy. Actually joy is the precursor of the event that one usually thinks is the *cause* of the joy. As we have said in the prior chapter, healing only needs an intention that is held long enough to outwait all of the doubts and fears. Thus, it is by means of an intention that an individual is healed in their aura, receives the healing, and feels joy. Then the body healing occurs, followed by happiness. Indeed, it is a conundrum that everything that is in existence now, was once only a thought, followed by an intention and given some time to materialize, but it is so. And so with the flashing light of joy going off on your dashboard as an indicator of your healing, let us proceed with an explanation of the role of joy in the human experience.

But first, we heard you ask another question. What was it that you were thinking just now?

Joyce: For me, relationships make me either joyful or miserable, mostly the latter. I'd like to ask about the most intimate of all relationships, that between God and ourselves. How does God create? How did God create me?

Hathors: If you will allow us to address this question, we will give you the rendition that was used by the ancients who brought Egypt to glory. Yes, indeed, the Creator giving life to a creation is the first and original relationship of love that gives form to all others. So for the moment, let us go to the analysis of what creativity is. Remember when you created that quilt square? Do you remember the happiness of giving your thought existence on its own and looking at it with satisfaction? When you create something, you feel happy to have replicated something beautiful that was within you so that it has an existence of its own. Once one realizes that one is a creator just like the original Creator, then there is no mystery as to why God created, only how.

Now let us suppose that one who had lain asleep for a long time, awoke with a dream of how something could be created, just for the love of creating it, and set about making it happen. Then, let's suppose that the creation, say a statue of a lovely person, comes alive and talks and loves back. Would not the creator be amazed and pleased that their creative idea could be so powerfully put into place as to have intelligence, will, and love for themselves as well as the creator? Much like parents giving life to a child, creation is very satisfying.

Now let's suppose that those who choose to have children, have the same experience, yet their knowledge is limited as to how. They only know the why. They want an image of themselves that walks and talks and loves them back. Would they not want to participate in the how by huddling together, planning, and making all things good? Then when it arrives, would they not give it all that it needs to be happy? Thus it is so with God. Having arranged every breath of your life, God rests in peace that it will go well. This is the true foundation of your confidence in your life being good.

Furthermore, if one assumes that the created one has a separate and independent free will and can choose to return the love or not. The return of love freely given is a great satisfaction indeed.

For God is the only being that exists in all of His many forms and all who are created are still within the confines of the body of the Creator.

Thus it is that all who were originally created as souls had existence as a flurry of activity within God, going in circles round and round and then condensed into orbs of existence with life living within them. But they never left God, the womb of their conception. In fact, the universe of galaxies had the same experience. God just got bigger as the joy of creation caused more and more creation, which only made God more joyful. It was the joyfulness that made God bigger, thus able to create more. It is the same for you.

Therefore all of creation was made for the joy of it and exists in the love-giver who created it and keeps it in existence. That's all there is to know about yourself in order to feel safe in your existence. God made you because it made God happy to do so. So how does that make you feel?

Joyce: Safe and secure and joyful. And I now view all other beings as co-habitors or fellow cells in a huge body. Hello, over there. Remember me? You treated me *sooo* mean in that last lifetime, so now what do you have to say, knowing that you live along with the rest of us in the amniotic fluid of our mother/father Creator? You feel foolish, I suppose. Well, get in line with the rest of us and take a big drink from the umbilical cord of life coming from God, as we all get fed the same and are made of the same stuff and have nowhere else to go. Possibly we can get along better now?

Peaceful One: Only possibly? Don't all cells work together for survival when one is damaged? All seek to heal the cells in trouble for the good of the whole, which is good for each cell. This is just what Christ taught, by the way. Does it sound very much like our definition of the Highest Good?

Joyce: Point taken. So if God is the only being, is there such a thing as something outside of God?

Hathors: We will address this question because so much more knowledge of how the Godhead grew into vast proportions is requested.

No such thing exists if its name is non-existence. But for a long time ago as to be acknowledged as extinct, there was a field of existence known as darkness that is no longer in existence. But for that to be explained, we'd have to go back to the story of Egypt.

For in ancient Egypt, there were those who did not know or live in the realm of Egypt. They did not know how good it was, so they lived in their own world, which was bereft of peace. Occasionally, one would return from a long trip and make mention of Egypt, but few would make the trip to find out for themselves. Thus it was the same for those in the cosmic range. For some beings existed in a form of compromise for a very long time. But then another form of God was created to express the traits of love and wisdom and came to be so great, that all others joined that entity not because it was so big, but because it was so benign and wise. Thus all came to know and love each other as beings of peace in love with themselves as cells in the body of such a great being.

Joyce: Are you saying that God has many forms? I thought that God was a single, eternal, never created, and never ending being. Please explain.

Hathors: Within God, there are many forms of God all created from its own stuff. Yes, indeed, God did exist for all times as do all souls, but time is a physical plane phenomena. In spirit form, God keeps expanding and expressing Godness in many different forms. Godness feeds all beings with such great love, it opened its perimeters to be invested with the weak and the wise, the good and the bad and none was turned away. As they basked in the light of such love, they were made whole and one with their Creator and thus they became creators as well. And so it was done over and over. In fact, there is a long line of such creations stringing back to so long ago as to be forgotten even to us. Much like the tip of an iceberg or a slip of mountain pass, there are many gods to be had, all of the same construction and kind of existence for they are all one. They all reside within the great Godhead or source of Godness.

So do not forget to ask us more about how God expressed His goodness over and over again, for these same patterns will emerge as the peace project heals the Earth.

Joyce: So I take it that there's much more depth and existence through growth within God. God is a many layered or sculpted, being constantly unfolding, replicating, and expanding. It does not surprise me that it is greater and more beautiful than our Conscious Minds could have devised.

But you were making the analogy of cultures all over the world not knowing the peace that was resident in Egypt. Did you mean to imply that there were beings that did not know God and when they came to know love, that they willingly joined God? And God took them all in, healed them, prospered them and they become part of God. Am I right?

Hathors: How right is right? But if the left turning universe is to be seen as a way for one to hone one's own existence by choosing to turn to a better one, then true it is that those in the right turning universe assembled so many that they took over the whole ground, which is what is about to happen here on Earth.

To relieve your tortured mind, yes there was an original Creator, but God is typically referred to as the manifestation of love and so it is that love acquires more and grows and expands as it exists. It cannot be resisted. Thus we find that the great entities, teachers, and souls of grace are like God marketers. They invite and instruct all who wish a life of peace, where to go, and how to get inside the God space of their hearts and stay there. It is a process that happened on the spirit side as well as on the Earth.

Once there, typically none leave, but some did and are living on the Earth plane and are about to return to God in great kind and numbers. And that is where we began so long ago. For humans were once the kind that lived within God and had a Higher Mind to live there and remain. Then in a moment of time, some turned and left to discover what else was present. In doing so, they needed no introduction to the horrors of the Conscious Mind for it was resurrected from the distant past and left to prosper as it might. That they may be made whole in as fast a time as is possible, they were allowed to remain in existence as Earth-bound souls under the care of karma which is a quite painful, but quick teacher of the value of the Highest Good.

Age after age transpired on Earth in which the Conscious Mind was made to rule and then decline. With each decline, it was all the more difficult for bad to rise.

For when much bad is followed by much good, much more good is desired and no one wants to give up any of it. Thus we find that, at this time, mankind can more easily choose to not leave God.

Joyce: So, were all humans of the "leaving God" kind?

Hathors: Yes, but for different reason. Some who never left God have come to reshape human history over and over again. Finding more and more converts, there are the holdouts who have been in reversal for so long, that they are duty-bound to never end on an even keel and need much drama and malicious intent to pave the path to their redemption. We were sent here long ago to help both parties, for we also never left God and never will. Thus we are the source of great patience, wisdom, and caring about each and every soul no matter their deeds.

Joyce: Does this have something to do with right turning, then reversing to left turning like you said about spirals?

Hathors: What would turn left would be of the intent to leave and discard what is good. The right is to accept and to amass what is good.

Joyce: Just like "righty tighty" and "lefty loosey" for tightening or loosening a screw?

Hathors: So it is for keeping close to the Highest Good. There is the story of the seed distributed by the farmer who would be God. God came in many forms to convert holdouts into becoming returnees, thus the story only ends with the good. As the leavers become returners, they bring back many experiences not only of pain and suffering, but of grace and redemption, thus they are to be honored. For they will become the impassioned leaders of those whose Word is to be God and no other. They might be thought to be explorers rather than rebels, as they return with many fine resources to be shared by all. Therefore, some come and some return all of the time until good becomes too vast and strong for them to leave. And some, being in a weaker field of energy, can leave and will not return for a very long time. Thus the story continues on.

It is essentially a love story. God loves boy and girl. Boy and girl get lost in the woods. God goes to find them and brings them home. Then boy and girl have children who get lost in the woods, so God sends His son to fetch them back. It is an etcetera kind of thing with many variations. It is the way of free choice beings. In fact, there are villages or families of wanders and fetchers and they all get along very well, happy to do their duty to the Father who raises so many children.

Joyce: Interesting, it sounds like a community of people who have culture, roles, and rules.

Hathors: Interesting it is, for some who have made it back have so much to say that they have to recruit those in physical existence to take notes on it back to the physical realm. It is a sort of back talk. That would be you, by the way. Now, would you like us to return to the story of Egypt?

Joyce: Yes, but it will take me a minute to get used to the idea of the vast God who creates another God who becomes vast. It must be like a large spiral organism, or a rose that opens and exposes yet another petal. Oh, I get it. Each of these Gods is a Dimension Master, right?

Hathors: How right you are depends on the definition of God. All who live in the divine peace are God, but yes, there are Godheads who founded a certain form of consciousness that is eager to form its own culture of Highest Good. They are each given a deed to their own dimension. Christ is the deed holder of the Earth's Green Dimension. As your landlord, He wishes you to all show familial love for each other and tidy up your home planet a bit.

Joyce: Oh, that is funny, but so simple to understand. Well, we best be cleaning up our act. OK, so now let's go back to Egypt for it was called a golden culture.

Drawing 7: Egyptian Image of The Hathors

Hathors: A very long time ago, we came from a community (dimension) of Godhead to Egypt and asked to be admitted into the human community living there as helpers of civilization to be benign. And so we were admitted and have been there ever since. You can see our etheric faces carved on ancient temple columns, but we were always in spirit form and needed people willing to open to communication with us to speak our wisdom. Without ado, we rejoiced and spoke to all who would sit still and hear, saying that all is well within the body of the Creator. All who come and go in consciousness have nothing to fear but fear itself. Thus there is no feeding one a blessing without feeding another and so forth, for all swim in the same amniotic fluid connected by cords of attachment. As the Great Creator smiles, then all of the Gods are rolled in laughter and groan with the desire to create yet another and another form of God. Then they all expanded as the Creator expanded and shared their group experience so that all might be admitted into the wonder that is God and God and God, etc.

As the ancient Egyptians came to understand that this was their universe, they began to build a society on the same premise. They were known to say: "Let no man come into my kingdom and stay, without leaving as a better man." And thus it was, because it was taught that there was nowhere else to stay or go, but in the belly of a Beloved Creator of many beings of grace. Being founded upon this one truth, there are the paintings on the walls of tombs and temples of their many beautiful visions of peace. For example, here are depictions of people who come ugly and in grief, but who leave perfected, healthy, and happy. Over time, they honed this type of society and all visitors experienced the same grace.

They even wondered if future generations would ever believe that such a miracle really took place. So they made depictions on the walls of tombs and temples, in plaster, stone, and masonry. They all tell the same story in many variations. Such was the gift of the man who came to be the savior of all mankind and the God of the founder of this civilization. It was the Christ Consciousness, the master of this dimension, who guided the Revered Healer to exemplify one simple truth: You are living in an Egypt that is within the God, who founded the Earth and all of the stars, so rejoice and be made one of mind, heart, and body. For none could be made whole without total confidence that God made all to be benign, and thus it would be so.

For some, it was an evolution of thought development over time, and for some it came suddenly as an awareness that all are one, even a snake or a spider or a crocodile. They even depicted themselves as half human and half animal in appreciation of a trait or gift that the animal expresses in cooperation of their own. With this idea of oneness, those who sought to be separate were never given a chance to succeed. They were so nourished and gifted by the whole community that they became convinced that they would never succeed without the efforts of the whole community. And thus it was so.

Do not think that it was a form of communism, for it was in reality a form of Oneness, funded by people helping people. From that frame of reference, the unity of the one and the whole was sensible. Many came needing to be cured of illness, grief, and faults. They were given the best healing yet to be practiced on the earth. And with such loving care they were perfected and, with that gratitude, devoted themselves to the common good, knowing that to do so was their part of the grace of the union.

For the society to succeed, it needed to be based upon self-love, and thus it was described as a more perfect union, giving one the opportunity to be in pursuit of one's own happiness, only to find that it was also the happiness of all others. Yet none were neglected or short-changed in the least. This marvel of social engineering was planned at the highest levels and we would like to refer you now to him. It was he, the Revered Healer, who founded this society so you can ask him how he came to know that this was the true path for himself as well as for the nation.

Joyce: What a privilege! I get to hear from the Revered Healer.

Revered Healer: I am perfectly glad to be referred by this name, as I never found a single person or situation that was not improved by being healed or cured. Healing was and is my passion, just as it was that of my twin soul, known as Edgar Cayce in the recent century and who lived later in the great society of Egypt. For we were so imbued with the desire to teach the world that all can be cured, that we left no doubt about it.

In Egypt, when I needed to do or to be something, I simply asked to be healed of the limiting thought or emotion that would not allow me to be or do so. And in doing so, I was asking to expand, just as God the Creator has done so many times. And in expanding, I began to incorporate within myself all of the blessings that I requested, both for others and myself. So why would anyone want anything else than to serve others in this manner is the question? I considered the idea of exclusivity to be positively ridiculous and thus I have returned over and over to make do with less than the best, only to find that nothing I lacked could ever make me less and everything that I gave to others, made me bigger, finer, and happier.

When you pray for more benefits of being alive, you not only bring the benefits to your local participants, but you also give God a great laugh of enjoyment being able to create yet another happy offspring living within the great heart of the Creator. Thus the fulfilling of a request is yet another part of the love relationship between the Creator and the created. The more love that is created, the more joy and laughter rolls through the whole being of grace that is the Creator.

Joyce: This is amazing. I never thought about still being inside of God – all of us all of the time. And to think that it includes all of the galaxies and all time and space. Somehow, I assumed that God was elsewhere and we were outside of God trying to get back in. What a foolish drama that is. If we are always inside of God, then we have nothing to fear and a great deal of happiness to enjoy. We have nowhere to go, nothing to learn, nothing to perfect or to strive for. We could just ask for all that is good and be grateful for the good and it would only expand. We could follow the example of the Revered Healer and ask that the limiting thought or grief be healed, and be willing to expand with the happiness that would follow. Our only activity would be to further express our version of Godness in experience after experience.

If we have chosen to experience the lack of something, then we have the opportunity to ask for the fullness of it so as to experience the reverse. The resulting joy would be very intense which would only expand us further, and God with us. I wonder, how vast is vast?

Peaceful One: Let us congratulate you on the definition of grief, which is to believe that one is deficient. This should be the true definition of sin. Repentance is to find that the fullness has come through love. Indeed a fine thought. And in thinking such a thought, one must wonder how thoughts have entered into the equation at all. For if one lived within a giant mass of protoplasm, wouldn't each part be governed by the thought of the whole?

Joyce: That is a good example of a leading question that is sure to give a great insight. So individual thought: How *did* that come about?

Peaceful One: How could a doer of the Highest Good be in doubt about a problem when there is no thought of separation? For separation is not a reality, but only a thought. It is a thought that was thought at first by a fallen angel and has not until now been discovered to be the foolishness that it is. For a thought to have any value, it must adhere to reality and separation is not a reality. No other thought but Oneness would create the Highest Good. In fact, such false thinking is the source of so much pain and suffering as to be proverbial. So do not ask what is wrong with thinking, rather ask, if a thought is grounded in truth or not.

Joyce: I see your point. So are you going to answer your own question?

Peaceful One: Unless you would like to answer it for me, as you are so wont to do these days. So how did you come to seek the resolution of all of your thoughts into only those that were real?

Joyce: I could see that my life based on my past thinking was not going very well and I wanted to get to the bottom of it. I wasn't sure what I would find if anything, but I knew that the thinking I was using was wrong. Is that what most people do?

Peaceful One: How could one doubt such a one who came and gave so much good as to provide you with health, good friends, money, and a peaceful place to live? Just how good was that?

Joyce: Very much good, and no harm. This is the age-old definition of the Highest Good.

Peaceful One: Well, then let that be the measure of how much your thoughts are guiding you in the right direction. In addition to that, the need of one to be in charge of another and to give them guidance in the right direction could be governed by the same criteria.

For example, how could a police officer tell his arrested one that this is a good time to look at his life and find where the good is in his criminal actions? How could a schoolteacher find her student crying from bullying, and ask how could some good come from the situation? What could the student learn that would guide him or her in the future? How could a manager ask his employees how they could be more productive without working any harder, but yet earn more for the company and themselves and their families? Such conversations are the stuff of the future for some, but for others it has been going on for a long period of time.

Joyce: Well, that is what we teach at our client companies and there is indeed much that is good which comes of it. In fact, employees look forward to these conversations as it implies that they are valued and productive ones becoming even more so. Sometimes, however, the positive changes come slowly, even though they have staying power when they do materialize. Yes, these are thoughts in the right direction and even if the results are slow to come, they are so worth it.

So let's get back to the topic of joy. If I am living in the body of God and God is good and God is love, then I would only have good and love to experience and only the thoughts of fear and pain would deny me that. That gets me back to the beginning when I decided to not pay attention to the Fearful One. The thought of trusting the Peaceful One was true to my reality, so that thought was right and all else followed from that one moment. This is really simple in some ways, but profound as well. It was always there, I just see and understand it better now. Sure took me a long time, but then, it was time well spent. Nothing else really matters, unless it is me getting the chance to ask more questions. Hold on, there's more.

Chapter Seven: Gift of the Stones

Joyce: As I listen to the alto flute music called *Never Forgotten*, I am reminded of how this music emptied my heart of grief and make me feel secure and loved during times of trouble. I think that I felt the Presence of God in that melody. Tell me more about God and the feeling of God.

Peaceful One: How can we tell you much when he who needs no introduction as the Son of God is so near?

Christ Consciousness: "How near is God?" is much the better question. For dear one who cannot be forgotten, you are so near to me as to be an inclusion in my very being. My every moment is made possible because you exist and continue to love and to breathe. Do not make me lost in a fog of prejudice and definition as most religions do. Why not just let the emotions feel the emanations that are lodged within the aura glowing white and whole, and notice that some energies are coming and others are going. Thus the whole subject of assimilation and elimination is ended, for it is merely the breath of life and once started, it must continue. Thus we were never parted and never will be. Just keep breathing in the air, the sunlight, the fragrances and aromas of life on Earth and you will be able to emerge from this experience in full form and function.

Joyce: I can see that I am in the middle of a living being and enjoying the same life giving coming and going of energy and I can see that all of us are the same. So therefore, I sit here entranced in joy and cannot even move. For the moment, there must be something of a shift in awareness going on. For where would I turn to find more or why would I accept less? Is that the point of all life, to just be in the midst of life and be carried wherever that life takes me? Is it just the fun of two, being one and conversing as to what best to create next? Would that this be duplicated all over this world, so that all can rest in peace and go about living a happy and productive life.

By the way, if our auras are a mix of many colors, what color is God?

Christ Consciousness: If we had a consciousness to even conceive of the beauty of God, then the presence of such a One would be awe inspiring. Just let this little thought take hold in your mind: How much loving energy does it take to fire the stars with explosive energy, feed untold hearts with love, wash away the tears of generations of victims, and to build the premise of peace in such far-flung parts of the galaxy? That is the grace that is God and no less than the best part, is that you are a part of it all. Not just in the commanding presence, but because you wished to appear as one or another and to find your own place and identity once again.

So what color is love and what love can color the sky, the great abyss of space, and the fiery center of the sun? Let say all colors, for all are one and the same in the white light of golden tints that flirt across the sky of your aura at times like this.

Just imagine how long it has been since mankind knew of its being in such clear definition and wise guidance? Why do you come and do this, my greatest one of record keeping? Do you do it for me or for you or for all of us? Or do you do this because there is joy in it and you cannot get enough of it? You hunger and thirst as a way to describe the acquiring of so many beautiful experiences for each is yet another nibble, swallow, or indeed intercourse with the one who made you to be just like Him. So let's just be in one another's company a while longer. Later we will take a break for a meal and one long last look at the Egyptian landscape to see for yourself why all of the statues were smiling with peaceful faces and arms and legs at rest. Did they not know how to form this presence for the whole community and enjoy all of the benefits that it would bring?

Joyce: If how I feel now is any indication, there must have been community-wide bliss. But how could this be created and maintained?

I cannot think about ancient Egypt unless I think about the Revered Healer. He founded the whole thing by teaching the principle of the Highest Good. Then he taught each one to release their fears so they would be healed. I can see how refusing to think thoughts of fear would cause one to avoid illness and even to perfect one's body. I like the idea that we all exist within God and that our auras surround our bodies and hold the thought and emotional fields that can either nourish or starve us of Divine energy. I realize that our aura fields intermix somewhat and that we share our energy with each other. But all of this does not explain how a great culture was developed by one man sitting on a sandy plain with a few followers and nothing much but the intention for the Highest Good.

It takes a lot to influence an entire culture with a lot of people, some of whom might be warlike or at least angry. At least that is my experience. There has to be something that he used to create this culture that I've not heard yet. So, Hathors, you're on. Give me the whole story, please.

Hathors: Since this is a very long road to travel and involves the very creation of the universe, let us use a form of shorthand or we will be very much older than we already are before we are done. With your permission to be short on detail, but long on truth, we will proceed with an overview of how it all fits together.

Summary Reading of Human Auras and the Plan for Peace: Peaceful Societies

Peace and Light Association
Peaceandlight01@aol.com
PeaceandLight.net

As you were so glad to find out, God creates by expanding and forming new life within Himself. Since God is good, all that is created and resides within God is also good. And being a living organism, God is made of energy, so it is safe to say that all energy comes from God who gives it with joy from within the Godhead.

With that said, the nature of energy is to be in motion. In fact, all energy is in spiral motion, which rotates round and round, in a giving or receiving direction, each having a purpose. For instance, some spirals rotate faster than others which is measured as frequency. Each frequency has specific characteristics.

In addition, the motion of energy can be clockwise (Right turning, giving, or RT) or counterclockwise (left turning, receiving, or LT). Thus, there is always equalization between spirals, from one giving to one receiving. When giving and receiving occurs, great energy is released in the form of charged, energetic bubbles that contain energy to give. These are called orbs and can even be photographed under certain conditions. These orbs are generated by RT spirals and float freely until captured by a LT spiral needing a particular type of energy orb. Some orbs have a very short life, but some are the focus of great interest and intention and can solidify into physical objects or living beings. That is how the orb that is the human aura creates the human body. An energetic ball of energy is formed and concentrated intention is applied until a human body is formed. After making a body, the orb then maintains, repairs and even remanufactures another one when necessary. This orb is essentially the human aura.

Sun

Earth

Drawing 8: The Human Body in Its Aura

All energy comes to the human body through the aura. The aura holds the thoughts and feelings of the body and the type of the thought and emotion in the human aura is important, as it can distort the condition of the human body, creating illness and disease. Thoughts and emotions that can be brought into peaceful alignment with the original design of the aura, which is good, will lead to health and well being. This cooperation with good is described as forgiveness, but it can also be thought of as opening one's mind to more good in the form of a peaceful thought process.

Orbs have consciousness and always make the decision to act for the Highest Good. Orbs can be given intentional direction. Orbs holding intentional energy and aligned in a specific direction form the phenomenon of magnetism. Lined up in a single direction around a physical object, the magnetic field of orbs can give off electricity. In this case they are cooperating in conscious group intention. Thus electricity is the consciousness of the Highest Good in group action, so to speak.

The human aura has a magnetic field of energetic components around the human body, which represents the soul's attachment or relationship with it. Within the human aura are many spirals of both directions and much exchange of energy takes place as some spirals take in energy and others give off energy. The entry and exit points are called chakras. The constant giving and receiving of energy creates a composition of orbs within the Human Aura; each electromagnetically charged to be doing some good. In the Human Aura, orbs bounce around like balls in a cage until one is needed to fill a gap within a spiraling vortex. Thus none of the many needs of a body ever go lacking for an instant, unless there are no openings wide enough to accept the required orb.

Thus the most damaging effect of fear is that it causes the human to doubt that good is being created and is always being offered freely for its good life. If doubt is present, there is no expectation of being helped, causing the spirals to close up, thus refusing the orbs that could bring needed life energy. The body is left to feed upon the existing energy within the body, effectively causing deterioration of the organs, bones, and muscles. By being closed, one cannot accept good and even worse feeds upon its own deteriorating energy. This is the definition of old age and illnesses such as cancer. On the other hand, by being open and confident of one's support, one can reach the highest of goods without delay.

A "reversal of illness" or "healing event," can be created by opening the mind and the heart to the possibility of help being available, as close as one's own aura. In a reversal event, tremendous amounts of energy are exchanged depending on the difference between the frequency of the giver and receiver orbs. Thus, those who try the hardest to be open, receive the most energy and thus healing. Doubt closes the spirals called chakras and its destructive effect is to stall the energy flows, causing depression. If this would occur, one spiral would exhaust itself by giving, followed by a new impulse to reverse and begin to receive, for there is so great a difference between the exhausted giver spiral turned receiver spiral and the new giver spiral. These reversals are part of the workings of karma. One action creates the same reverse effect in the receiver as was experienced in the giver.

Thus, some who have come to this planet to have reversal lives will be allowed to proceed to almost complete self demise so that they can reverse and form an even stronger opening for the good. This is the function of the cycles of golden ages followed by dark ages. These ages have been going on for a very long time and will come to completion when fear is overcome. At this point, the electromagnetism of good will have finally reached a level where it can no longer be denied. Thus there is the need to discuss the electromagnetism of good.

As is commonly known, the Earth has weak electromagnetic fields. These weak electromagnetic fields accumulate around ancient sites, quartz-bearing rock structures, and deposits. Although the field of energy seems weak, it is well organized and well balanced, and it can go on forever without any consumption of fuel. Controlling all of this flow of energy is the gift of the unique properties of the electromagnetically charged quartz crystal.

Quartz Crystal

If quartz were to be understood as a being coming to life, it would be said to be like a statue of marble having a form and image. Thus, within each quartz crystal is the image of a great maker of good. It is a carrier of intentionality for the Highest Good in many different forms of giving. In each case there are observable conditions in the stone, such as the cloudiness, the length, the angles of the tip and facets, and the multiple conjunctions of several crystals together growing into a cluster. Observing these features of a quartz crystal will help one to recognize the particular gifts of each individual quartz that are possible.

With that in mind, it can be said that within each crystal is so much harnessed power that they could be called Great Givers of Good Energy.

But, it is in the making of a weak electrical field around the crystal, that the inner image of quartz comes to life. By rotating some of its own power in a circle within itself, the quartz releases in a controlled way, the full potential of the power held within. For this reason, it is harmless but also powerful.

For full power to be released, a quartz, like any other atom, would have to be bombarded with sound twice the speed of light. But this is not at all necessary. Without much of any intervention, the quartz type of stone can give a simple, but profoundly beneficial gift. This is the system that was used by the ancients in their stone monuments and it is eternally the safest and most comfortable and convenient energy source on the planet.

Since the Earth has low frequency magnetic fields, which are close to the ground, energy can be sent long distances without disturbance of any kind, especially along ley lines. The Earth is thus amply supplied with all of the energy of this type that it will ever need to use. Just by collecting some of this Earth electromagnetic energy, one can create a very benign local environment.

Both people and plants respond productively in low-frequency magnetic fields. Once the production of food in each home is undertaken within the confines of a low frequency magnetic field as is created by active crystals, a year-round supply of vegetables can be counted on. The reliance on mass transportation of food is reduced.

All of this brings us to the need to have a reliable and constant supply of low frequency magnetism in one's home, which was the solution that most ancient societies used and found that it was productive of health, channeled information, productive plant growth, and peaceful lifestyles. The grand monuments were all constructed with quartz-bearing rock and pointed in the four directions or, if a circle, with a freestanding rock, circle, or core in the center. Many travelers who came to inquire about the effects, found that their health improved, they conceived robust children, their plants grew vigorously, their minds were freed from fear, and they could hear their gods speak to them. Thus they gathered near the monuments and prospered, evolving into great societies.

Thus it will be again, as there is a great need for the earth and her peoples to be at peace at this time. One can utilize the true nature of a quartz crystal to harmonize and control the flow of electricity. This reading has attached to it a description of the Quartz Henge device, which will be the beginning of the system. Once understanding of its effectiveness has been accepted, then the device can be improved by channeled transmissions. All quartz crystals are different in their abilities and the sharing of information learned will guarantee that all of their capabilities will be made available to all.

The function of Quartz Henge is to concentrate orbs circulating in a desired direction within a small space, creating a weak magnetic field, which creates energetic motion in the air above it. This motion gives an energetic RT spiral drawing from the higher energies to the lower. The human aura, entering into this exchange area, will release its lower energy orbs and absorb the higher energy orbs, thus healing and rejuvenation will occur.

As people gather, they will experience peace, opening to channel their Higher Minds, healing, rejuvenation, fertility, etc. In short, they will feel the bliss of the Presence of God. They will gather, just as the ancients did, to receive the many kinds of good that were generated around the great monoliths. To maintain these good things, they have only to avoid fearful thinking. In this way, a peaceful society will begin to be promoted. After many generations of such living, those who have been rejuvenated and live happily for a long time are able to teach others the technology and organizational approaches that worked to support so much good.

The essential functioning of the orb generator known as Stonehenge can be replicated on a small scale using quartz crystals, sand and a glass bowel. It will generate enough peaceful magnetic field strength to heal all who live in a home. Generation of such healing energy fields will allow many peaceful families to reform today's societies into a new peaceful golden age.

Thus we come to the end of this lengthy reading and encourage all who stop here to read, to explore for themselves the healing properties of such a device as the Quartz Henge. Vastly more economical than the health care system and offering no harm or discomfort, it is similar to the original plan for the Earth to be in harmony and peace. Amen.

+*+

Joyce: How astounding! I don't understand the science behind it, but I can see that if this could work that no harm and much good will be accomplished. I get how it is based on the fundamental spiral energy exchanges of the universe, but it would be within our local neighborhood of the Body of God. Indeed, it is replicated within our own auras, which is how it would heal our bodies. OK, this opens up a host of new questions, but let's take it step by step. Tell me more about how quartz crystals can be like Stonehenge. By the way, I like the name Quartz Henge.

Directions for a Quartz Henge

Reading: Ancient Stone Sites, 8.12.13
Peace and Light Association
Peaceandlight01@aol.com
Peaceandlight.net

Ancient stone sites were miracles of etheric engineering in that they were forms that let earth energies be concentrated in a way that enhanced the lives of the citizens living in the area. Ancient engineering found that, if the setting sun could be focused on the center stone of a stone circle opposite the rising sun in the morning, that the encircling earth energy would concentrate. Those who stayed within the circle for a few moments to a few days or years would eventually open to their channel and, after a long time, start to become younger and younger.

Once this building of stone circles had started and the benign effects were measured against the labor to construct the mechanism, it was quickly learned that those in high places who gave the instructions were indeed benign beings and needed no introduction to the earthlings as anything but gods. Therefore, these sun-based monuments were viewed as being solely responsible for the raising of the health and welfare of the great civilizations.

In particular, those advanced Highest Good practitioners and etheric engineers at Stonehenge never left their bodies without the promise of return. Their agreement was that after death, that they would be returning in a new body and lifetime, in only a few years to resume their work. Then it would be known that their ancestors were indeed themselves, now reincarnated. Soon it will be understood that they left their bones in certain places as markers for their return so that they could once again build such sites. But until their return in great numbers, much smaller projects will serve as models and demonstrators.

With this knowledge, we have the bridge into tomorrow created. For once it is learned that the stone circles were indeed communal channeling houses of great strength, most if not all in positions of power will want to duplicate them. Channeling houses vary with the times and technology used in a civilization, but today they can be constructed with a simple container based on similar plans as were done in the past.

A likely small model would be a meter or less in circumference and be a perfect circle with no intervening airwaves between the standing pieces that form the circumference. All edges of the standing quartz stones need to touch so that the connections are complete. As the sun arises, the stone, crystal, or even concrete basin collects the sun's rays on the opposite side of the circle from the rising sun due to the fact that it bounces back and forth forming a recycling current which eventually moves around the circle to form a column of charged air particles that have electricity of a very weak kind. As the ground resisted the flows and the sun accelerated them, the energy rotates and amplifies. As this air column rises, it recirculates round and round the form until it advances past the horizon, carrying static electricity or charged particles out into space. With this spiral shape, the Earth itself which is charged with the energy of the sun reflected and recirculated back and forth, forms magnetic fields so that even on dull days, the sun's rays creates a weak polar effect around the stone circle. This peaceful energy calmed the weather and enhanced the natural features of the earth.

This crystal generated polar effect is in no way dangerous or harmful, in fact, it elicits a feeling of euphoria, which is the hallmark of the Highest Good or the Presence of God. With enough time spent within the area of this circle, one would be able to consume vast amounts of energy orbs from the device without harm, thus allowing the body to reshape and reform itself into its original perfect design. Thus we find that Joyce's farm is dedicated in such a way that a round circle is formed around the Christ Consciousness portal rock thus allowing the people who come to be transformed into power generating stations themselves. They receive and later give away the benign Christ energy to others to use.

A simple Quartz Henge device is constructed as follows. Obtain a selection of quartz crystals about 2-3 inches long and place them in the sun for several days, turning them to the right for several minutes each day.

Bring a glass bowl about 10-15 inches in diameter, half-filled with sand. Perform this Sand Ceremony using a series of containers each a bit larger than the one before. Fill the smallest with sand and tell all assembled that this small container was like your heart, small and empty. Then God filled it to overflowing. Explain that you felt gratitude and opened your heart bigger (take a container of a larger size) and God filled it, too, with blessings until it overflowed. Do this four times until you feel very blessed. Your gratitude will be absorbed by the crystalline sand.

Return the sand to the larger Quartz Henge bowl filling it about half full with the gratitude sand. Place several quartz crystals, about 2-3 inches in length in the sand, standing tip straight up in the positions of north, south, east and west. Then complete the circle of crystals with other smaller crystals until all are touching and the circle is complete. Anoint the circle with a small amount of oil, pouring it over the crystals and between them to make a strong connection.

Then place a candle in the middle, light it, and pray for the light of the consciousness that graced the earth in ancient days to come and inhabit the little circle. Once that consciousness has reached its destination, there will be a pale glow of pink or red that will briefly go around the circle. Blow out the candle and remove it. With this done, put a small bowl half full of water in the center to replace the candle in the middle.

If needed, place an upside down larger bowl of non-conductive material over the original bowl as an umbrella to protect the device from rain. Leave it outside with the east stone facing east, etc. Wait several days to a week or two as the cycle of the rising and setting sun moves energy though the device. The resulting orbs being produced and traveling in a right turning spiral form a weak magnetic field, which creates a Right Turning spiral and orb above the device, drawing down higher energy.

It is recommended that one remove the cover and take an energy bath each day in the energy orbs. These orbs have two properties. As the rays of the sun are transposed from one part of the circlet to another, it will create a transmission of grace that both draws out grief and brings in grace, thus creating the rejuvenation and channeling function of the circle. With this done, there is no need for anyone to worry, as it need only be placed outside for it to be effective. Indeed it can be placed upon a tray and brought from one area to another as needed. It would be a simple and inexpensive task for each home to make and use this device, as quartz and sand are available in all parts of the world just for the picking up on the ground.

Although there are many other designs with the same purpose and function, for now, let it be understood that even these small Quartz Henge circles, will be an effective means for the reformation of much that is good. Amen.

+*+

Joyce: Well, Dear Reader, if you haven't yet made one of these, then you are not as curious as I am. I found some crystals and used playground sand in a glass bowl. I did the sand ceremony, which was very moving. I lit the candle and prayed from the bottom of my heart for the Christ Consciousness to come and live there. I then replaced the candle with a small bowl of water. After leaving it outside under a cover for a few days and nights, I then brought it in to enjoy an energy bath. I noticed that my houseplants are growing profusely near it and I feel a strong sense of bliss and happiness at home, that I don't feel when I leave. As I let this device expand and grow, I would be very interested to find out what other good comes.

Oh, by the way, I know that you are probably thinking about the Great Pyramid, which was not a circle like Stonehenge, but probably had much the same purpose, so let's ask. What about the Pyramid and the Sphinx?

Hathors: Such excellent questions. Let us address the question of the Sphinx, which was an effigy of the Revered Healer as well as a rising sun energy collector. Also, what is the difference between the energy created by the Sphinx facing east and that of the circular form of Stonehenge and others?

To make an analogy, if one were enjoying music of various kinds, one would have to realize that although they are the same notes, each collection of notes is organized in a harmonious form of melody and rhythm. Thus the forms of the statues and monoliths create quite different energetic effects.

For the Sphinx to be understood, one would have to know that it was created by the intense labor of just one man adhering to the intention of the Highest Good in all thoughts, intentions, and labors for the sake of his people. This one man was not just a man devoted to his people's good, but was a partner with the cast of thousands in the spirit realm who healed his heart, body, and etheric body into one that could challenge the great minds of any generation before and since. With this one mind in constant unison with the Highest Good, he surrendered his Conscious Mind with ease and made no further reference to himself and, rather, referred to the mental body by a name meaning peace and contentment. Later depictions of him show him to be a humble and kind man using only one hand to form the path to peace.

It was with his single-minded dedication to the Highest Good, that he acquired his ability to read the cosmic code in great detail. With this ability, he led his people into the chambers beneath the ground to plan the building of the Great Pyramid thousands of years before it was begun. With the Highest Good of the earth in mind, he needed to form a monument of intention that would last a thousand years, reminding all who came that there was much more afoot there than a sea of sand.

Thus he founded upon the idea of reshaping a small mound of ancient seabed floor that protruded from the plain. This was the first mastaba, which was a natural feature, but served as the primary promise of what was to come. So indeed, thousands of hours of labor was invested in cutting and carrying stone from around the emerging lion body to be placed in front of the paws in the shape of a temple of standing energy-catching stone. Later the upper body and head were formed from blocks of stone. By facing east, the stones and the face of the lion would catch the rising energy of

the sun and transmit it into the national energy
monument that it has become.

Therefore, there is a question to be addressed.
How did the Sphinx function not only as a reminder of
this great man and his intention, but also as a gatherer
of energy to fuel a peaceful economy capable of
planning and building the Great Pyramid? With one goal
in mind, at first one monument was built and then later
a more massive one. The face of the Sphinx looked east
and its tail extended toward the west pointing the way
to the position of the foundation of the pyramid to be
built thousands of years later.

With one sand creature having been built, there
was a need for another. Fortune would have it that the
grand temple at the feet of the sphinx was needed to
reflect the energy of the sun in the correct direction so
as to accumulate a great ball of energy that hovered in
the sky over the Sphinx. For this to be seen, one must
look with the mind's eye, but the image of two lions
back to back with the sun disk between them on the
dream stela is a sample of what most people saw when
they inquired.

Drawing 9: Orb over the Sphinx

This orb of light was of the size of a temple wall with unlimited power to transfix the populace in the gifts of the Highest Good. For anyone who entered into the compound with faith would eventually find himself or herself invested with great strength of mind and body. And if they stayed long enough they would be energetically transported in mind and body into the pyramid chamber, well into the future, to be refitted with a new body of light. This new body would be one of perfect intention, grace and charm. It would literally never die and could perform feats of great strength such as lifting tall stones to be hefted into place, such as is depicted in yet another drawing of the sphinx showing the two lions with an obelisk between them.

With such men, much could be accomplished that would typically take a team of thousands to perform. Thus to those having the will to proceed, the means was provided. These people were called the Great Ones and would be considered the fifth race of mankind, not made from the first kind, but wholly constructed of the truth of their aura. Both male and female were included, for many were the women who beheld themselves as they ought to be, not as they were, and wanted to bear children of like strength to further the race of such humans.

This orb or disk was an intentional being, capable of recharging the human aura and whisking away the debris of regrets and grief. Once one devoted oneself to its care and keeping, the entire population benefited from its presence. This care and keeping consisted of setting the intention daily to be in the Highest Good and nothing else. Indeed, each event of each day was interpreted and transmuted into a function of the Highest Good, such as is depicted in the Bread Oven drawing in the Book of the Dead. This drawing will be given and interpreted in a future book. Thus, the outcome of the reflected energy of the rising sun harnessed to the intention for the Highest Good gathered much energy of the earth's rotation and rolled it into a ball of sorts, which would hang in the air above the heads of the people. And so the lion was a symbol of great strength that lay silent and relaxed but powerful.

In the case of Stonehenge, there was no need to be symbolic. By that time, the great Sphinx was legendary and there was only the need to raise the great orb of enlightenment and then to live in its glow long enough to absorb the energy into one's aura and thus be healed and made strong. The people would collect at certain times of the year to do homage to their trust in the Highest Good which had done good for them and never bad and to bask in the glow of its emanations.

Thus it comes to mind to ask, why there is not the same energy orb to be seen there today. By means of mental picture forming, one can still see the faint outline of the original orb, but without the constant forming of the intention by the populace, it has diminished and faded. With more interest in the cosmic body of grace at the Egyptian plateau, there will be those who come to wholly devote themselves to correct intentions that will reform the original orb of light so that the population can enjoy the benefits once again and begin to understand the value of the monuments that still remain. With the strength of knowledge and body that the orb can give, they will return to the prosperity of peace and build a strong society that can be admired around the world and rebuild much that has been destroyed. With this accomplishment planned, there is much to do, but one does not need to depend upon these events to occur, to benefit from the same effect on a smaller scale.

That brings us to the nature of the winding spiral giver that is being called the Quartz Henge device. Should one find oneself with one of these in their home or business and consistently build the orb themselves with the intention for the Highest Good, then the small orbs generated by the crystals will come together and begin to expand and strengthen until a mighty one of great strength resides right along with the residents. It will fuel some amazing feats of rejuvenation, health, beauty, and strength.

There are those among the readers of this book, who are looking for those who can read the cosmic record and provide such information in a reliable form. They come with open hearts and minds and are decidedly interested in spending their days and nights in the company of the orb and its creator. Thus there will be found among them, those returnees who came to participate in this undertaking. With this group assembled, the Mystery School of modern times can be founded. And with much to do that is to go right and little wrong, there is much that is wonderful.

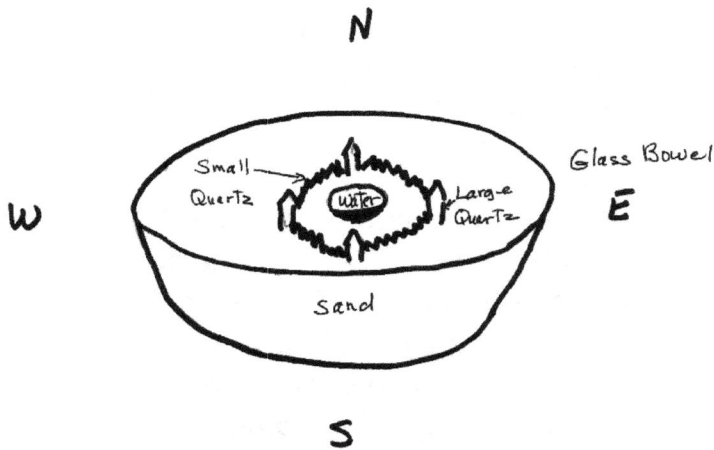

N

W   E

S

Drawing 10: Diagram of a Quartz Henge

Joyce: This is all starting to come together is a beautiful way. I can see why the Peaceful One started me out with trusting the Highest Good and told me to place a small quartz crystal on my crown chakra each day while asking for the Highest Good. According to this reading, I was taking the natural orbs generated by quartz and accumulating them for my own use in my aura to accomplish the Highest Good in my body and life. Yes, It is a slow process, but now I see that on this less than grand scale, it created a golden age for me.

Dear Reader, do you want peace to be your byword and thus enjoy a golden life under the small sun of your own energy orb of grace? Then you will do so, for all that it takes is a few small things and the intention to do so. So simple a thing done in a timely manner makes good for all of us as well. So I wish you prosperity, health and happiness beyond measure knowing that all who live with you will experience the same. You are your own monument to peace, even if you don't look like a lion of stone.

Chapter Eight: A Plan for Peace

Hathors: With this chapter completed, there is nothing to achieve by more readings than to be certain that there is indeed a universal plan for peace. Indeed the earth can be seen as but a small part of that plan, but from where we view it, this is much the same plan everywhere, only different in time, place, and a few details of historical record.

So, let's destroy all fear, jealousy, conflict, anger, depression, and illness and leave behind nothing but peace, prosperity, and happiness for every being on the planet. No other plan has been made but this one, and for it to succeed there is only a little bit of wonder to behold and commitment to be made in favor of the good and to ignore the bad. So that others can understand, we will outline its process in better detail so that all can follow its form and outline and revel in its completion.

First, there is the need to be sure of the plan's benign conception. For, from the beginning, there was no need for any to be in the physical plane unless those that came become aware of their status as a creative being of grace. Thus, to make this clear, it was designed that they would be able to create all that they wanted, even the good with the bad. By having established that, there are those who insist on being given more bad than good who have to learn that they can be reversed to the good at a flick of a thought. When this has been thoroughly experienced by each individual, then all has been completed for this passage of time upon the Earth. For the Earth has been an experimental station of sorts and has served its purpose well. For the present, there will remain both kinds of experiencers, but soon those of the bad will be leaving and not returning. They will be reversing into other forms of life, not being able to incarnate on the Earth again for the time being. This is the purpose of the peace plan. For if enough of the residents of the Earth community wish peace, then none of the opposite may apply and survive. Their existence will continue, but not on this planet.

The peace plan generally is thought to be a campaign or conquest of territory or even minds, but this one is literally a conquest of the heart. By heart, we mean the mind and emotions that exist in the aura of a human. Should these areas of the aura be peaceful and no longer churn with grief, regret, or anger, then there is total acceptance in the outer layers where the Contented Ones can be contacted and the Great Oneness admitted to the earth for their vast gifting of grace. Should even one or two achieve this level of peace, and yet one more join them, the battle is essentially won because the energy that is created is such that it cannot be denied and will spread like wildfire until it consumes all in peace and love.

Thus we have come to the end of a long progression of light and dark periods upon the Earth and the many who have travailed so long are at long last assembled, incarnated and ready to do the peaceful deed in such vast numbers that the world will be transformed just by their existence. Therefore, we have no more words of wisdom than to recommend that you take the time to remain peaceful in all experiences of your life and let your aura heal enough to admit the truth of your being. For it has only been the small but confusing barrier of conflicting thoughts and feelings that has caused the pain, suffering, and grief for so long. And, in doing the exercise of adjusting the current economic flow of goods so that all can enjoy access to a simple but good living without conflict or undue labor, there will be many more who wish to do the right thing. Many inventions of the simple, but profound kind will be introduced and made available for all to see and use without limitation of any kind.

Thus the stone circles of ancient times will have done their duty, for even today they are sending the right message in very weak form and with a little redoing, they will be recommissioned with great glory as many people need the supportive help of the great stone monoliths in their communities. Indeed, the regular method of preventing all manner of grief will be to go to the garden and resurrect all manner of stone of a crystalline nature and lay them in a circle and then sit and meditate on the goodness of nature. With such simple but powerful techniques, much good will be done and none will be lost to harm.

With this, we wish to remind all who have come to this point to be glad that the planet will not be blown up by a nuclear explosion, nor crashed with a meteor, for none such event was ever in the plan and never will be. None but the presence of the Christ Consciousness is at the controls and one and all can know Him and His purpose by his life in Galilee. So for the present, proclaim nothing but peace, both within yourselves and in your families and communities. And for this, He has said before: "My peace I have given you. Go and make peace in your own heart."

+

Dear Reader, I can see that our goal is to make peace in our own aura, hearts, homes, communities, nations, and environments. It sounds like a big job, but it starts with us. Do you see, as I do, that the very first experience was all about that? The clear message to trust the Highest Good and to ignore the Fearful One was indeed the first step. It was also all of the steps in between and indeed the last. Although you might think of forgiveness as giving in to those who harmed you, the process of forgiveness is not about right or wrong. It is about self-acceptance and refusing to live in fear, anger, regret, and guilt. By refusing fear, you keep it out of your aura where it can do so much harm and replace it with the intention for the Highest Good which can do so much good. It occurs, when you open to the possibility that you are loved by your Higher Mind in a way that you cannot understand, but that you can trust. It means that you will begin to experience good, not fear. You are refusing fear and insisting on peace. You are refusing to be ill and rather choose to open to all levels of life giving energy. To make peace in your own heart, we needed this private time in which to converse, you and I. But in this third book, we find that it can easily echo around the world with profoundly beneficial consequences.

Do you wonder what was meant by the power of only one or two hearts operating out of peace? I think that it has to do with keeping the mental and emotional layers of the aura calm and in harmony with the outer layers of Contentment and Oneness. This barrier of thought and emotion was the only barrier we ever had to deal with, after all. The fears, angers, hurts, jealousies, grief, and depression are all of our own making and that means that we can unmake them ourselves. Once we do that, then the formation of a strong orb over our crown chakra comes automatically. This orb has the power to both protect and nourish us with all of the life energy that we need. How strong is yours? How strong is mine? You can see it with the inner vision of the mind. Just ask to see your own and let it pop into your imagination. This is how Medical Intuitionists do it. We can do it too. Do you feel it? It feels like bliss, confidence, security, and, of course, peace. How does one create an orb like that? Keep the intention for the Highest Good constantly in mind and work with it in every circumstance in your life. Ignore the fears and release the emotions associated with them. Could it all be so simple as that? Let's finish with a talk with the Peaceful One.

+

Joyce: Dearest Peaceful One, I have talked with you consistently for five years now and I've always called you The Peaceful One, but I never understood how important that name is. I suspect that you are the outer layers of my own aura where peace resides in the connection to the Contented Oneness. I connected with you when I calmed down my fears enough to bring my mental and emotional layers into harmony. Indeed you and I are one and we are both in peace now, for I will never allow my fears to ever disrupt our harmony again. I'd miss you too much to let that happen.

Peaceful One: Will never again do for you? Will it do for all others who seek peace? What will they do? Will they labor on in dread, fear, depression, and sorrow lifetime after lifetime, or will they hear your words and savor their experiences so as to learn from them?

Joyce: I set the intention that all readers experience their Highest Good, when I started this whole thing. I asked for the Highest Good for the whole project and all associated with it. I lovingly conversed with Dear Reader and those who are reading now have made it to the mountaintop of truth. Gratitude is in order, which of course, creates joy. Our Readership orb must be way juiced up with joy.

Peaceful One: Just so, for joy only serves to enhance the orb of light that you are. And with that, there are so many ways to be in love with yourself. There is nothing within or without that can harm one so protected and nourished.

Joyce: So be it for Dear Reader, and may each additional reader enjoy the gift of peace more profoundly each day, giving the same gift to all that they encounter and thus it will travel throughout the world. We have unleashed the explosion of peace and it turned into soft, flowing, peaceful light. Sweet.

Have I told you lately how happy I am? I love you so much.

Peaceful One: Me too and Dear Reader makes three and then several billion more. Anything else we can do for you today?

Joyce: No, I think that will do for today. I am in awe of myself, a Being of Light. Dear Reader, I give you the following gift and all of the blessings that will follow from it.

I give you my gift of peace.
Go and live in peace and give it to all others.

Preview of the Next Book:
Book of the Highest Good, Volume 4:
A Channeled Tour of Egypt.

Joyce: So much has been disclosed in this book that I would think that you, Dear Reader, would have to take some time to think about it and ask many questions. I know that I did. But such was not to be the case for me for long. As my mind traveled to Egypt, I pondered the pyramids and wondered about the wall paintings and hieroglyphs. And then there were the funeral customs. I watched some history and archeology programs on these topics and away I went with the desire to get more information. I felt the urge to return once more to my desk and, of course, was greeted in bliss by The Peaceful One.

Peaceful One: We have called you to the computer screen once more as an act of kindness to the one who came to speak to you as Great Giver. He would like to address you once again about the tombs and tunnels and their use. For following your viewing of the DVD, there was some consternation as to the true use of them and the conundrum of mummies. And so with your permission we would like to begin.

Joyce: Yes, of course. I suspected that the common understanding of tombs was only a partial story or at best, a guess. Proceed.

A Description of Ancient Egypt
by the Great Giver

As I stated before, there never was a royal class of people in my time. Although in later ages one did develop, I was not in favor of such. Indeed, every common man had the right for a mummified burial in a tomb of his or her choice. Those who had greater skills and served the community more had access to more knowledge and skilled laborers to negotiate more elaborate burials. However, none were paid more or less and neither was I. Indeed most people only received enough food and drink to support their current daily needs but not for individual stockpiles. All distribution of resources and labor was done by the administration workers for the benefit of the community.

At last, there is a reader with the common courtesy to allow us to explain ourselves in our own way and to create an understanding of how we lived so that many others may choose to do the same. We will start with funeral practices. At first, when a person died, there was a distinct difference in their appearance as death represents the withdrawal of the soul from the physical body, but we knew that the consciousness of the deceased was in the aura. We understood that the aura remained with the body to discharge the energy in an orderly way. Thus until this process was complete and the bones freed from the tissues and scattered, the soul was capable of giving the energy to another. And so the remains were wrapped in linen and dried so as to do no harm and much good. When the skin turned black, it then was time to inter the body in the ground or crypt. The form of the body was preserved in the coffin so as to be energized again in etheric form as the keeper of the person's memories and skills, which were of much use to the people. The people would visit the coffin frequently to give the departed one's soul access to their Higher Mind for the care of the people's needs. In short, they kept the bonds of Highest Good in place for the benefit of all.

The fact that the internal organs were removed and placed in jars was more for the respect of the portals to the Higher Plane that they provide. We sang death songs not to bemoan the loss of a loved one, but to heal ourselves and them from any remaining grief. We were very adept at remote viewing and scanned the body and the organs easily. As we scanned the condition of the organs for signs of grief, we healed them so as to allow the deceased to flow freely into an afterlife condition known as remorselessness or better stated, innocence. The funeral party participated in the last healing of the body because a healed body was a seal of the discipline with which the individual lived his or her life and by participating in the healing, and each participant received a healing from the deceased for themselves as well. This is how the Highest Good works. The family and friends would want the deceased and themselves to have the best and most wholesome condition for their soul's journey between the dimensions. Later, some mummies were even painted blue to signify that they were entering into the Blue Dimension.

With that cared for, there was the condition of the senses to consider, for the senses made entry to the Blue Dimension possible. The nose was the organ of scent, which was, for the common man, the way that the human body could best attach itself to its Higher Self. In short, one could smell the afterlife and follow the scent trail to the destination. Thus there was the image of the dog or jackal god, Anubis. The dog image was used because it can follow a scent to find its mate, its home or its next meal. Often, the nose of a deceased one was opened to the forehead, not for the removal of the brain, although this was done, but more importantly to open the sinus cavities as they were important for the proper functioning of smell. In the case of the deceased, it was the energetic sense of smell.

Later, cavities around the eyes were often opened as well using a pick so that even the sight would be clear. If an object was inserted in the place of the eyeball, it was an onion or a marble eye just for the effect of an eyeball. And so with both organs of scent and sight completely cleared of obstacles, the deceased was judged ready to be laid to rest in a tomb. Having been wrapped over and over again in linen, it was a long time before the body would actually shrink and decay, so much of the skin was in tact, but the muscle and viscera were gone. Thus the sense of touch was left in tact as well.

The mummification process was not just to preserve the body, but to also prepare the earthly representation of the soul for its journey into the afterlife where it would have to rely on its senses to find its way home to the Presence of God. Finding God is more an emotional contact than a place or a face to see and it needs to be done with innocence, not with shame or guilt. After that, all was left in tact for a long time before actual burial was done so as to assure the parties that there were no remains of grief to be cleared out or unhappy memory to be retrieved. The events of the person's life were discussed and healed by those who knew them. For example, if the person had an affair during marriage, their sexual organs would be washed and preserved in oil so that the toxic intention to forsake the Highest Good of the marriage would not deter them. In short, all was forgiven and the soul could go quietly to the next dimension with no shame as could be visible in the etheric body sometimes called the double.

Thus we come to the reason why so much gold, useable valuables, and food were left in the tomb. For such was not for the deceased, but rather for the blessing by the deceased for the use of those left behind. Now fully forgiven and blessed, the deceased was the ideal giver of blessings on the community valuables for the benefit of the community, so they symbolically left their items of sustenance for the blessing of the forgiven and beloved one to make to prosper. After all, one so close to God would be able to send the gift of the Highest Good to their Beloved Ones in physical form. Thus the community often returned to take some of the valuable items for the use of the people knowing that they were blessed with the Presence of God and thus the goods would prosper and multiply many times over. Thus such a tomb would play the role of a treasury of blessings or even an investment house with regular visits for the purpose of deposits and withdrawals as the people's needs required.

The reason why King Tut's tomb was undisturbed is that people wanted his treasure to remain in tact so that he could consolidate his benefits. This is because he lived a most sheltered life in Amarna as a retarded boy and given much in the way of resources as was the custom. Thus his remains were put to rest in a simple grave as he had little to give, but much to receive and few would be coming to visit. A small tomb was stuffed with the riches that he would need to draw from, then closed and sealed at the entrance with the sign of the Highest Good at work in such cases. Indeed all respected the sign for to enter and to take such goods would be a breach of the law of the Highest Good and such a one would reap much loss and misfortune. In short, to take his goods would bring down upon the taker much loss as was evident when it was discovered and taken into custody. With that we would like to say that the modern day discoverer of his tomb is in no way responsible for his own demise. By entering the tomb and taking the treasures to a museum with the right intention to serve the needs of the world to see and understand the tomb, all good will follow the treasures. The consequences follow the intention, not exclusively the objects.

Thus there is much more to be found about the customs of we, the ancient Egyptians, that is nowhere else to be described, and we allow for the grace of yet another book to be formed so as to give much more information. But let it be said for now, that the principle of the Highest Good is alive and functioning strongly in this work. For should this reader have selected any intention save that of the Highest Good, nothing like this would have been given. The strong intention for the Highest Good is so in harmony with that of the Great Giver, that he makes himself known once again by his own adage. "Give me a stone and I will serve you with bread."

+

Joyce: I think I would have enjoyed being with the Revered Healer and this Great Giver. I would always remember the peace and goodwill. What a wonderful way to live they present. I wonder what effects it had on the local people as well as the rest of the ancient world. Oh, now I just cannot stop. I have to start the next book.

Will you join me there? And yes, I will not forsake the intention for the Highest Good as you can see just how important it is, not only for myself but for all others. Let's make a pact, you and I. Until we meet again on these pages, keep that intention close to your heart, as I know that you will heal and prosper in so many ways as to be legendary.

So long for now and forgive yourself for all and everything. That way, you can keep your body and all of its parts clear and clean of the toxic effects of grief. I wouldn't like to see your heart in a pickle jar with all manner of grief visible to anyone who looked. After all, your heart could be happily in love with your Higher Mind. There, that's better. Forgive all and live happy. Until we meet again, I give you the gift of peace.

Resources

Peace and Light Association

It is our mission to help others to open to his or her own Higher Mind Channel. As these books depict, everyone has two minds, a Conscious Mind of daily physical life and the Higher Mind of the Soul. The Conscious Mind engages in fear and its manifestations such as anger, depression, jealousy, and conflict. The Higher Mind lives in peace and gives health, guidance, and access to all other Higher Intelligence. You can only get to your Higher Mind if you are in peace and intend the same thing as does Higher Mind: The Highest Good for all. Once you practice the skill of contacting your Higher Mind, you can ask to be given directions for healing all aspects of your life and helping to solve the problems of a society in conflict. Reference: *The Book of the Highest Good, A Beginning Experience*. Also look for: *Book of the Highest Good, Volume 2, Walk to Freedom*, By Joyce McCartney. All are available at Amazon.com.

Reading on Health: The Higher Mind surrounds the human body with an aura that is like a womb, feeding it, healing it, developing its full abilities and protecting it. It is called the Body of Light. The chakras are the entry and exit points of the assimilation of such light and life giving energy (clockwise turning) and the elimination of pain, grief and illness (counterclockwise turning). The chakras can be closed with doubt and fear or opened with faith and joy. This is the role of forgiveness, to release the pain and open to the joy. The body of light is where the connection with Higher Mind occurs and if you open to your Higher Mind, the guidance will lead you step by step to open the spiral tubes of life energy and you begin to actively engage in the giving and receiving of the Presence of God which is your destiny. If you develop a daily practice of relaxing and opening in peace to Higher Mind, then ask for a daily reading of personal guidance, and you will be given all that you need to prosper and much more. You will be given the blissful Presence of God.

Contact us at: Peace and Light Association: peaceandlight.net and peaceandlight01@aol.com

Intuitive Musician: Phil Crabtree: phil@peacepiper.net.

Listing of fears which cause specific illnesses:

- *You Can Heal Your Life* , by Louise Hay
- *Heal Your Body, A-Z,* by Louise Hay

The Long Story

This is a very long story that I am about to tell you, and it is essentially a love story.

So settle in for a view of how love created a world of peace.

In the beginning, as it says in the Bible, there was God. And God loved being the great thought of love and the Source of all life. There was God and nothing else. Everything was in peace.

In one great moment, God wanted to love someone else, and so created many souls in a great act of conception. This is who we are. We are those souls. We were created from the substance of God to BE LOVED and to be companions in the giving and receiving of love. We were created out of the substance of love, for that is all that there was or is. In fact, we never left God. God just expanded his borders, for us to be part of him. So you can see that love is our nature, the same as our Creator.

Later, God wanted us to be able to love back as beings of thought and action, and so a universe of places to experience life and love was created in a big bang. The stars, solar systems, and galaxies appeared within God. In fact all physical existence is still within the body of God. We entered in spirit form into these places where we experienced many things, sharing them with God, always coming back to the appreciation of how much we were loved.

We loved giving love back to God and to each other and created many beautiful experiences including procreation. At all times while we were in physical existence, we existed in spirit form as well and enjoyed the Presence of God, which was very peaceful, blissful, and safe.

Being in the peaceful Presence of God is our Highest Good. In fact, we have to be peaceful to fully experience the Presence of God.

In spirit form, there is no separation among the many souls. We are always in total and constant communication with each other and know every thought and experience that any of us have. We also know the Mind of God, for we are of the same mind. Being with God and each other is our only desire. This is the Greatest Good that we can ever have.

In this spirit form, we are known as the Great Oneness. And we, the souls created by God, live as ever-changing orbs of light in peace and security, having no fear.

When we came to the Earth, we found animals and plants and became interested in the experience of living in a physical body. The DNA of the hominid form was developed as the best vehicle to house the great mind of our high souls. We wanted to be creators like God who gave us life, so we created a smaller version of our great Soul Mind and experienced living with this small, undeveloped mind; essentially a baby mind living in the human body. We refer to it as Conscious Mind and with it we fully experience physical life. The Soul or Higher Mind, being in spirit form, experiences everything at once, but the Conscious Mind can only know and experience things one at a time because it lives in time and space.

The Conscious Mind is a very limited version of Soul Mind but is of the same construction and ancestry. It desires to be loved and to know truth, however, living in time, it learns in steps and does not always use its free will wisely because it does not know the whole truth at once. These Conscious Minds needed to learn to deal with the Higher Mind through cooperation, much like a teenager learning to drive a car.

For each individual, after each lifetime, the Conscious Mind was brought back to the soul. The life experiences were reviewed so a decision could be made about having another lifetime to increase the cooperation between the two minds – and thus achieve the destiny of the Conscious Mind to "grow up" and be in complete cooperation with Higher Mind. When this is achieved, both enjoy the Presence of God as wise and loving souls.

Thus, human kind developed with two minds, the Higher Mind of the Soul and the limited mind of the Human Conscious Mind. It was a very confusing experience because the two minds were quite different.

The Higher Mind channeled only the love of God, but the Conscious Mind did not see the whole picture and thought that we were all separate. It could not recall who it was, why it was here, and where it was going. It did not remember the Presence of God except as a distant yearning, so it often chose fear, anxiety, depression, conflict, greed and aggression as a way of life.

These experiences of fear proliferated as more and more humans populated the earth and the belief in fear and separation became part of all human experience. As societies developed, some discovered the fact of the two minds and were able to access both. Others emphasized only the Conscious Mind and participated in war, greed and cruelty, thereby creating poverty, disease and vast amounts of human suffering.

These fears became a way of life, as one civilization followed another – some better, some worse. Thus, human history was fashioned from these two minds at work on the earth.

It was mainly the great spiritual teachers who talked about the Higher Mind and its trademark feeling: Peace. They led the way to a better understanding of the human condition. They taught how to access the Higher Mind for that precious guidance of how to be safe and peaceful.

Peace is so clearly a characteristic of the Higher Mind that it is the password needed to enter it, and the lack of it is a sure sign that we have left the Higher Mind and are now operating in fear, which arises only from the Conscious Mind.

Thus, we come to the love story of you and your soul. You are one of those souls, a great Being of Light, living in a physical body with a Conscious Mind, possibly confused about the experience of the two Minds. You seek the faint and happy memory of the Presence of God available in the Higher Mind, but see the evidence of fear all around you in the structures of civilization and so doubt its existence. Sometimes you feel the peace and love, and sometimes you don't. You want to have that peace all of the time but don't know how to achieve it. So you become a hesitant seeker of your first Lover, God.

Fortunately, we have the great teachers to guide us. One of these was Edgar Cayce, who, in deep sleeping trance, spoke from his Higher Mind and gave readings. All of this evidence of the benign reality of the Higher Mind was to help us to understand and use the access to the Higher Mind, bring the Conscious Mind to wisdom, and to find our way back to God's Presence. The information from the Higher Mind is always directed to the Highest Good of all beings, meaning the Presence of God.

Cayce demonstrated that Higher Mind can retell the history of the Earth, give technical solutions to modern problems, suggest healing remedies, give great guidance for a better life and much more. Wouldn't you like to be in that peace and love of the Higher Mind more often? Wouldn't you want the unique wisdom of your own soul guiding you through your daily life experiences, unerringly taking you back to the loving Presence of God? Wouldn't you like to be free of fear, depression, anger, and grief?

There is a very clear method for moving between the Conscious Mind and the Higher Mind, and we will teach you that method now. When you are finished, you will have one small message from your own Higher Mind guiding you back to the Presence of God in small daily steps. It will involve bringing your Conscious Mind into cooperation and finding that the Higher Mind does indeed lead the Conscious Mind to a much better life. Thus you can lose all sense of doubt and fear. If you ask for a daily message from Higher Mind with the Intention for the Highest Good, it will bring you back to happiness, which by necessity would include better health, fortune, prosperity, social life, and relationships.

These messages are from your soul, in cooperation with all of the other souls who are in constant communication with each other. They assist anyone who asks by responding from the great stores of information on everything that has ever been experienced by them. You can communicate with any soul that you wish, including those who have passed over, just by asking.

You can receive guidance on many problems and projects, even highly technical ones. The Great Oneness has a sense of humor and a gentle loving way of helping and teaching us. They are the network of mind, the fabric of space and time, and they would love to help you because you are one of them, a part of the Great Oneness.

Here's how it works. First you must be peaceful, because that is how the Higher Plane works. The minute you are in doubt, fear, or conflict, you revert back to the Conscious Mind, so we will do a short relaxation exercise and use some imagery to get you peacefully started. The next thing is to set the Intention for the Highest Good and nothing else. After all, you wouldn't want anything else for yourself or anyone else.

Finally, see yourself as one who is loved, waiting for someone who loves you, to communicate with you. This one who loves you is content that all is good and that nothing of harm can come to anyone including you. Then you can ask away. Begin a journal for your notes, and all that is for your Highest Good will be given to you and nothing else.

Keep in mind that it is never in your Highest Good to be frightened, criticized, judged, or sacrificed for anyone or anything else. You are to be treated with nothing but love.

There is no guilt, judgment, or punishment, no matter what you have done. There is only loving help. Such fearful and negative thoughts can reside only in the Conscious Mind and will not manifest unless you chose them with intensity. Since you are not going to be listening to them for a while, you are in for a nice experience. Go ahead and give it a try.

Relaxation exercise: Sit as comfortably as you can and take three long, deep breaths, each slower than the one before. Imagine yourself floating on a soft cloud with warm sun and fresh breezes, and just rest and listen. The cloud supports you in perfect comfort and security. Then let the Intention for the Highest Good come from your heart and see it bloom like a flower all around you. It is soft, but very strong. As you look around, you notice others floating on their clouds. One especially nice cloud comes close to you and a hand reaches out to you. You reach out to touch the hand and suddenly you know that you have found your Higher Mind. Once you are there, let questions come to mind and listen for an answer, accepting whatever you get, a feeling, a song, an image, a word or anything at all.

Ask another question and wait for an answer. Do this over and over again until the process gets clearer and easier to do. Keep notes in your journal and see the progress. The most important question will always be: What is my Highest Good today?

Remember to refrain from judging what you get or doubting yourself or your readings. Just do it again and again. It will get better and better.

Test your readings with these questions: Does the giver of this message know me very well? Does the giver of this message love me very well? Is this message free from any fear or doubt? If you get a "no" on any of these questions, you are not fully in the Higher Mind. If you get anything fearful or judgmental, ask to be given true loving help. Keep trying until you get a "yes" to these questions all of the time.

And now we will let you rest on that peaceful cloud and listen to the guidance of your own Higher Mind. Take three long, slow deep breaths, rest on your cloud and listen to someone who loves you.

Acknowledgements

As the author of this most unusual book, I would like to acknowledge the pioneering contributions of other channeled works. Each author who had the courage to both contact their Higher Minds and to publish it to the public has made a very personal contribution to us all.

Therefore, I mention first and foremost, Edgar Cayce and his legacy organization, the Association for Research and Enlightenment (ARE) in Virginia Beach, Virginia. In thousands of documented individual readings, this humble man unleashed the vast resources and love of the Great Oneness in modern times. Most of the readings were for healing, but others were about history, metaphysics, and reincarnation. Without his work, we would have been strangers to what was so easily available to all. Contact: edgarcayce.org.

Since then, other authors have stepped forward with their own access to Higher Mind. These include:

Neal Donald Walsh: **Conversations With God**

Paul Solomon: **The Readings of the Paul Solomon Source**

Jane Roberts: **The Seth Material**

Gordon Smith: **Developing Mediumship**

Sonia Choquette: **Soul Lessons and Soul Purpose**

Esther and Jerry Hicks: **The Abraham Material**

Tom Kenyon: **The Hathor Material**

In regard to contact with nature, I make note of the work of David Spangler and the Findhorn Project.

I am grateful for the work of these and many other authors and greet all who are yet to come.

— *Joyce McCartney*

www.ingramcontent.com/pod-product-compliance
Lightning Source LLC
Chambersburg PA
CBHW071438090426
42737CB00011B/1702